Volume I

GET YOUR GROUP ON

Multi-Topic Small Group Counseling Activities

By Stephanie Lerner, MS

ISBN: 978-1-59850-219-0
Library of Congress: 2017956266

10 9 8 7 6 5 4 3 2
Printed in the United States of America

Project Layout/Design by Melody Taylor/GraphicSolutions, Inc.

For information on this publication or others by this author, visit www.youthlight.com
or e-mail the author at bilinguallearner@hotmail.com.

DEDICATION

This book is dedicated to my Del Valle Middle School group members.
Through the years, you have taught me more about group counseling than any
textbook, college class, or theory. Thanks, DVMS Students, for coming to
group every week with open hearts and open minds!

ACKNOWLEDGEMENTS

A huge burst of thanks and love to my sweetheart, Tommy, who took over 90% of
the home and ranch chores while I hunched over my laptop frantically
trying to meet my deadlines for this book.

I also have to give a monster shout-out to my parents who support all my wacky ideas and outrageous
adventures with a kind word and a wry smile. Whether it is flying off to Australia at age 19 to visit a
friend I'd just met, working as a Montana horse wrangler for the summer, joining the Peace Corps, or
signing on to teach English to Bolivian orphans in the Andes mountains, Mom and Dad, you two are
always the wind beneath my wings.

For Bob and Susan Bowman at YouthLight, thanks for giving me the chance of a lifetime.

Like and follow me on Facebook and Instagram, respectively, to see weekly posts on counseling
adventures and on the latest counseling resources!
www.schoolcounselorstephanie.com
www.facebook.com/schoolcounselorstephanie
www.instagram.com/schoolcounselorstephanie

Introduction

Purpose of this Book and Topics Covered

Get Your Group On: Multi Topic Small Group Counseling Guides Volume I provides counselors/leaders with a blueprint for planning and facilitating three topic-based psycho-educational groups. Readers will learn various strategies and activities that they can use in their own group sessions, as well as techniques for continuing to support group members after the group ends. This book will also address how to compile group data to advocate for future groups with campus stakeholders. The following counseling topic guides are included in this volume:

Girl World
Girl Empowerment,
Leadership, Friendship,
and Conflict Resolution

Boys' Voice
Boy Empowerment,
Leadership, Friendship
and Conflict Resolution

Be Cool!
Anger Management
Goal Achievement

[Note that reproducible activities for each session can be found at the end of each session plan and in the digital files available online at youthlight.com. Also, note that items identified as being in the Appendix can be found in the digital files.]

What is a Psycho-Educational Group and Why Run One?

Psycho-educational counseling groups are an amazing tool to support children and teach them the skills that they need to thrive. This type of group helps members to gain information and develop skills for challenging situations through education-based techniques. In psycho-educational groups, the emphasis is on teaching and learning, the group activities are structured, and the content is group specific. During group sessions, the counselor usually facilitates discussions of the material while the members build skills to overcome problems, share coping skills, and develop behaviors to successfully navigate new or difficult situations. The benefits of running a counseling group are invaluable – resulting in decreased symptoms of anxiety/depression, a better quality of life, increased knowledge of mental health issues, better access to community resources, and improved self-esteem (Lukens, 2004; Corey & Corey, 2006). For all of these reasons, I love running counseling groups and am always looking for something new to learn about and to try out in group counseling sessions. As a result, I have spent many years compiling and creating extensive, best-practice group counseling resources. It is my wish to share these resources with you in this book.

> The benefits of running a counseling group are invaluable – resulting in decreased symptoms of anxiety/depression, a better quality of life, increased knowledge of mental health issues, better access to community resources, and improved self-esteem.

And Now, a Word from *Luis...

Before we jump into all the details for running various counseling groups, I'd like to leave you with this story from one of my group members that will illustrate the power of group counseling. A few years ago in a group session, we were discussing how we all came to be at Del Valle Middle School. Luis, a tiny, very serious 6th grade boy who had been granted political asylum with his family, matter-of-factly told us about how he'd had to cross a large, deep river by hanging onto a tire to enter the United States. As we all gasped and asked him how that experience had gone for him, he described how he had been really scared because he couldn't swim and the water was up to his neck and all he could do was hang onto a tire and kick his way across the river. Then he triumphantly announced to us that he'd made it and took a deep breath before continuing on with his story. He revealed that he used to have nightmares about his crossing experience, but now that he was with us in group, he was feeling so much better. He explained that his nightmares and bad memories of this crossing had been replaced by feelings of pride because now he focuses on how bravely he crossed the river all by himself.

Luis' story illustrates what group counseling does in every session- it empowers students to turn the negative in their life into something positive. Being a school counselor myself, I know how hard it is to fit all the group planning and facilitating into your busy, busy day. So, I thank you on behalf of all the children you help through group counseling!

name changed to protect his identity

Recommendations for Starting a Counseling Group

To help group members get the most out of the group experience, I offer the following best practice recommendations for starting your groups.

» Included in this book are three counseling guides, each with eight 50-60 minute sessions. Each session can be easily shortened by omitting some of the activities if you have less time for group sessions or are working with younger group members. In addition, the sessions can also be lengthened by adding in some additional activities provided at the end of each counseling guide.

» In each of the three guides of this book, a group description is provided followed by tips for the counselor. Then a lesson plan for each group session is provided. After each lesson plan, reproducible student worksheets and resources are included. At the end of each group guide, general group forms are compiled in an Appendix for easy reference. The Appendix items are included in the digital files.

» Four to eight members is an ideal number of group participants, with some groups needing to stay closer to the four member mark and other groups that can easily be expanded to eight (or even ten) members. See the recommendations section in each guide for further guidance on this topic.

» It is best to meet once per week in a quiet, private room or area.

» This small group curricula was developed for group members in grades 6-12 in a school setting, but it can easily be modified for use in a clinical setting and for use with upper elementary students. Below are some tips for using this guide with elementary students:

  » The counselor/leader reads session passages aloud while the group members follow along with their finger.

  » Shorten or simplify some of the lists/cards in the sessions.

  » Have group members dictate writing activities rather than writing on their own.

  » Create a template that members can copy rather than writing on their own.

» Substitute an Additional Activity (provided at the end of the counseling guide) for any session activities that seem too mature for elementary students.

» Sometimes older group members might act like they are too mature or "grown up" for counseling activities. For these situations, just keep in mind that the counselor/leader sets the tone for the group session; therefore, if you are enthusiastic and comfortable with the activities, your older group members will be too. Likewise, if you feel awkward, juvenile, and self-conscious about certain activities, the students will mirror these feelings.

» This is a psychoeducational sessions guide. It should be used to educate students on mental health and wellness information and strategies. It should not be used as a substitute for mental health therapy with a licensed practitioner.

» It is important to screen members for inclusion in the group before the group starts. An effective way to do this is to begin with an informal needs assessment given to teachers and school staff. An example is provided following this explanation. You can also modify the example to use with students and parents. Have defined expectations for the students in group; these expectations should be based on data. Determine data-based group criteria that students referred for group counseling must meet in order to be enrolled in a group. For example, your group criteria might be "student is failing at least 2 classes" and/or "student has at least 3 discipline referrals," etc. Meet briefly with each prospective group member individually to discuss the group topic/purpose. If they are interested in participating in the group, give them the permission form (included in Appendix) so they can take it home for their parent/guardian to sign and return to you.

Hello Staff,

The School Counseling Office will be starting counseling groups_____.
We can run the following groups as needed: Empowerment, Stress Management, Anger Management, Academic Achievement, Grief & Loss, Changing Families, Exploring US Culture for Newcomers, Conflict Resolution/Making Friends, or Social Skills. Feel free to let us know if you have a suggestion for another type of group that should be offered. If you have students you would like to add to these groups, please email back the student's ID# and the group you'd like them to be in. We'd like this info by next Wednesday (_____) so we can start the process of screening prospective group members and getting parental consent.

Thank You, Your School Counselors

» Keep a Group Binder with a separate section for each type of group you run. The binder should contain your Group Notes sheet, students' schedules/teachers, permission forms (included in the Appendix) and any handouts you will use.

» Plan each session using the Group Notes sheet included in the Appendix.

» Both staff and group member pre/posttests are included in this guide. There is an explanation in session one for how to administer the group member pre/posttest (included in the Appendix). If you work in a school setting, you can also administer the Be Cool! staff pre/posttest (included in the Appendix) to teachers who work with your group members on a daily basis. It is best if you can attend weekly team meetings with the group members' teachers. I find that this is an excellent time to fill out the staff pre/posttest. Unless you work in a school that is very relaxed and well-staffed, I recommend against just e-mailing the pre/posttests or putting them in teachers' mailboxes. Instead, in advance of the meeting, ask for 10 minutes on the agenda from the team leader or head teacher. Then, during those 10 minutes, quickly fill out the pre/posttest with the team of teachers orally, writing down the number of their response, group-consensus-style. The staff pre/posttest, when provided, lends itself to this type of quick administration. I administer the staff pretest one week before the group starts and the posttest one week after the group ends. The goal is to see the numbers decrease from the pretest to the posttest.

» Each session ends with Discussion Questions. The questions are provided as additional opportunities to process or lengthen the session at the counselor/leader's discretion.

Recommendations for Leading a Counseling Group

In order to help your students get the most out of the group experience, I offer the following best practice recommendations for leading your groups.

» Demonstrate careful adherence to/reminders of Group Rules & Consequences (included in the Appendix) for each session, and post a printout of the Group Rules & Consequences in the group area. I firmly correct any group member not following a rule by gently asking them to read it aloud to the group. It is crucial to follow the consequence of having a private meeting after the group session with any member who is repeatedly not following the group rules. In the meeting, discuss the rule/s being broken and come up with a solution for following it. Remind the student of the solution right before the subsequent group sessions and the problem should fix itself. If the student continues to break the group rule/s, consider removing the student from group and providing counseling with them individually; in order to preserve the counseling relationship, it is important to explain to the rule-breaking student that they are not in trouble, but that their behavior is jeopardizing the success of the rest of the group and so it is better to work one-to-one.

Included in this book are three counseling guides, each with eight 50-60 minute sessions. Each session can be easily shortened by omitting some of the activities if you have less time for group sessions or are working with younger group members.

» Also, when you explain each of the group rules to the members, make sure special attention is paid to group rule #2 about confidentiality. Remember that confidentiality among minors cannot be guaranteed and this needs to be addressed with the group members. For example, I might say that we can't force anyone to keep confidentiality so it is important for group members to be careful what they choose to share in group.

» You might want to have warmup puzzles for group members to do as they're waiting for others to enter and the group session to start. This is especially helpful for the first session; group members often trickle in slowly during the beginning of the first group session because it's a new routine for them, so having warmup puzzles available will keep prompt group arrivals busy. Also, a fun and motivating puzzle is a great way to start off the group session on a positive note. You can find really good puzzle worksheets for free all over the Internet, especially on Pinterest.com. (Another good resource is 201 Amazing Mind Bogglers available for purchase through YouthLight.com).

» During sessions, make sure to work with students on whatever data-based criteria got them into group (such as discipline referrals, failing grades, etc.) - possibly through goal work.

» Use the group members' responses to the Group Evaluation (included in the Appendix) each week to plan/adapt your next session. You may want to laminate this as a poster so you can refer to it at the end of every session.

» During the first few minutes of a session, as group members trickle in, ask if anyone wants to discuss anything on their mind or from the previous week. In school settings, this is also a good time to address any discipline problems related to the group topic that might have occurred with a group member in the last week. Try to keep these discussions to no more than 5–10 minutes so as to not focus the entire session on them. If you feel that group members will have trouble staying within this time constraint, post the following guidelines on chart paper and review them with group members each session, as needed:

> **Group discussions are:**
>
> – 5–10 minutes (we will set our group timer)
> – focused on solutions, not problems
> – not name specific
> – helpful
> – serious
> – about group topic issues

» During the beginning of each session, it is good to review the optional homework assignment if you gave one during the previous session. Session homework is important because it allows group members to apply the skills they have learned and practiced in group. Application is an effective way to transfer information from our short-term memory into long-term memory, where we want group members to keep their group skills. Also, utilizing the homework feature and following up with it in subsequent sessions helps to ensure that the skills learned in group are reviewed and discussed in multiple sessions, rather than just covered in a single session. However, this review is optional, so you can skip it if the group session runs long and there is no time.

» There are a lot of read-aloud and sharing opportunities in these sessions. Always make sure to remind group members that they can say "pass" anytime they do not want to read aloud or share.

» If group members will need school passes to attend your group, here are some easy steps for making passes:

  – Get two copies of the student's schedule.
  – Cut/tape these copies together with the pass (included in the Appendix).
  – On colorful paper, photocopy half the number of passes you will need for this student, and cut the copies in half.
  – Repeat the three steps above for all other group members.
  – Paperclip a stack of passes together for each session, with one pass for each group member.
  – Hand out one paper-clipped stack on the day of the group session.

Recommendations for Ending a Counseling Group

In order to help group members get the most out of the group experience, I offer the following best practice recommendations for ending your groups.

» I find that collecting group data helps me to improve future groups and promote my program with school stakeholders (parents/administrators/staff). Included in the digital files is an extensive six-part data plan that allows you to present all aspects of your group's successes to counseling program stakeholders. Alternately, you can also compile and present as few of the parts as you want because data analysis and compilation can be time consuming.

» I have found that one of the biggest challenges in compiling and presenting data is actually getting anyone to look at it! Everyone always has more e-mails than they can read in a day, and unfortunately an e-mail on a bland topic like data will usually get overlooked. For that reason, I take all identifying group member information off my data and then post it in high-traffic, staff-only areas such as the staff bathroom (and usually on the wall right in front of the commode; it might sound a bit unseemly, but it works!). Since I started posting data in the bathroom, I actually have colleagues and administrators tell me varying versions of, "you know, I was in the bathroom looking at your data and I never realized that 60% of students' grades went up during your group" or "I was so impressed that Draco actually had 22 disciplinary referrals before your group and only 3 after!" Some other high-traffic areas to post your data might include: right above or near copy area, on the fridge right by the handle in the staff lunch room, or next to staff mailboxes.

» I often have a follow-up session about a month or two after the group ends to check in on group members' experiences/successes. To do this, I have included specific instructions in each group guide for how to run that group's follow-up session.

» At the time of the follow-up session, I also compile and analyze the After Group data (included in the Appendix).

» I have included suggestions for additional activities (included in the Appendix) if you'd like to extend the length of your group sessions past 1 hour or if you'd like to have more than eight sessions. You can also substitute any of the additional activities for a particular session activity if that activity won't work with your group member population.

» If you would like to learn more about any of the strategies or activities in this book, please refer to the professional sources listed in the references at the end.

Digital Files

Online access to digital files of all of the reproducible worksheets included in this book are available at youthlight.com. Simply enter the Library of Congress number listed on the copyright page of this book to gain access to all of the available files.

GIRL WORLD
Girl Empowerment Group Counseling Guide

{ Table of Contents }

{ Girl World Appendix }

Reproducible letters, forms, assessments and other materials contained in the digital files

- » Parent Permission Letter
- » Group Notes
- » Group Evaluation
- » Pre/Posttest
- » Group Rules & Consequences
- » Group Pass Examples
- » Data Analysis
- » Additional Activities

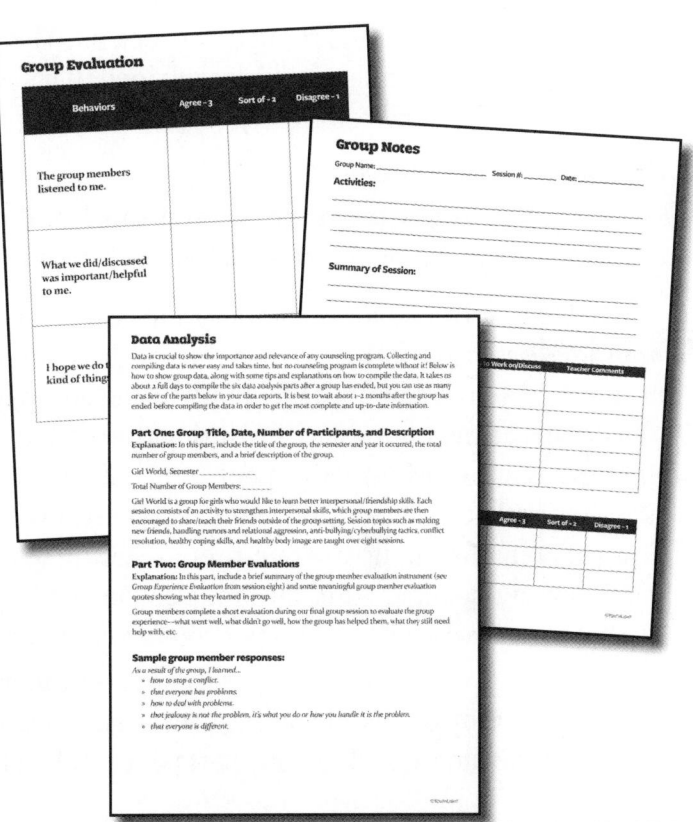

Recommendations Specific to Running a Girl Empowerment Counseling Group

Every year I run multiple counseling groups for girls to try and combat the Mean Girls culture that is increasingly prevalent these days. I carefully choose my group members for their strengths (which don't always present positively) and for their diversity in the various different school cliques. I do this in the hope that they will take what we learn in group and spread the lessons to their friends and family. To facilitate this, I pepper all of our sessions with little tidbits about how we are empowering each other through our group activities to go out and change the world—starting with their own groups of friends right here on campus. Every session, I challenge my girls to encourage, teach, and model how to handle interactions/communication with others (and the inevitable interpersonal conflicts) with grace and kindness. And every year, I am surprised again and again with how well this works! The success of this exponential model can be summed up nicely with the following anecdote. A few years ago, I was making my daily visit to the In-School Suspension (ISS) room to counsel my students who had ended up there because they had broken school rules. I came upon an 8th grader, let's call her Nellie, who 2 years prior, had been in ISS weekly. However, since attending our girls counseling group, she had managed to stay out of ISS until today. After she told me a bit about the behavior that landed her in ISS and we brainstormed some solutions for avoiding this situation in the future, I commended her on staying out of ISS for the last several months. Then I asked the million dollar question: "How have you kept yourself out of trouble lately when you were in ISS so often in the past?" Nellie narrowed her eyes and pursed her lips and thought it over a bit. Then she tilted her head, looked at me out of the corner of her eye and with a slight smirk explained that she stopped "talking mess" so much after she got tired of all "the drama" and realized in group that "some people actually take what others say personal and to the heart."

> Every session, I challenge my girls to encourage, teach, and model how to handle interactions/communication with others (and the inevitable interpersonal conflicts) with grace and kindness. And every year, I am surprised again and again with how well this works!

In addition to encouraging my girls to learn as much as they can in group in order to be role models for others, below are the practices that work best with all my different groups of girls.

» There has been an explosion in the last 10 years with regards to girls in the USA exhibiting self-injurious behaviors (SIB). Because this is a girl empowerment group, and not an SIB group, it is important to handle any talk of SIB during group sessions in a purposeful and careful way. If a group member brings up SIB during the session, gently remind the group that the focus of the session is on girl empowerment and guide the members back to that theme. Additionally, tell the girl that made the SIB comment/question that you would like to address her thoughts immediately after group in a one-on-one setting so you can provide her the best counseling environment possible. After the group session ends, meet with this student alone and proceed with her concerns/questions as per your organization's protocol for issues of SIB.

» During group discussion time, girls may have trouble staying within the time limits set- this can lead to the group discussion taking over the entire group session. To avoid this, it is a good idea to post the following guidelines on chart paper and review them with group members each session:

> **Group discussions are:**
>
> – 5–10 minutes (we will set our group timer)
> – focused on solutions, not problems
> – not name specific
> – helpful
> – serious
> – about group topic issues

» I often have a follow-up session about a month or two after the group terminates to check in on group members' interpersonal experiences/successes. During the follow-up session, I generally follow these steps:

- Take attendance on the Group Notes sheet (included in Appendix) and review group rules (included in Appendix).

- Ask group members what issues or recent situations they want to discuss relating to girl issues.

- Review the *Four Steps to Conflict Resolution* (included with session six), and have each group member select a relational aggression card (included with session three); the member can read the card aloud and then role-play using the four conflict resolution steps while the group leader (or a partner, if members can handle this) "bothers" the member with the relational aggression card behavior. Be sure to spend a minute or two after each role-play briefly discussing how their strategy could be applied in a classroom setting.

- Review the *Healthy Coping Skills* (included with session five) poster and play *Coping Skills Bingo* (included with session five) with group members.

» As mentioned in the beginning of this book, I have included Additional Activities (included in Appendix) for extension or substitute session activities. However, if at all possible, make some time to include the *Dear Girl World* activity from the Additional Activities section. This activity is an excellent way for the girls to apply their Girl World knowledge. It is best to include this activity in your final or follow-up session.

American School Counselor Association Standards Alignment

The American School Counselor Association (ASCA) sets the national framework for a model school counseling program. As a result, the Girl World session activities are aligned with the following ASCA Mindsets & Behaviors that can be applied to the domains of Academic Development and Personal/Social Development.

Mindsets

M 1.	Belief in development of whole self, including a healthy balance of mental, social/emotional and physical well-being
M 2.	Self-confidence in ability to succeed
M 3.	Sense of belonging in the school environment

Behaviors

B-LS 1.	Demonstrate critical-thinking skills to make informed decisions
B-SMS 1.	Demonstrate ability to assume responsibility
B-SS 1.	Use effective oral and written communication skills and listening skills
B-LS 2.	Demonstrate creativity
B-SMS 2.	Demonstrate self-discipline and self-control
B-SS 2.	Create positive and supportive relationships with other students
B-SS 4.	Demonstrate empathy
B-LS 5.	Apply media and technology skills
B-SMS 5.	Demonstrate perseverance to achieve long- and short-term goals
B-SS 5.	Demonstrate ethical decision-making and social responsibility
B-SS 6.	Use effective collaboration and cooperation skills
B-SMS 7.	Demonstrate effective coping skills when faced with a problem
B-SS 7.	Use leadership and teamwork skills to work effectively in diverse teams
B-SS 8.	Demonstrate advocacy skills and ability to assert self, when necessary
B-SMS 9.	Demonstrate personal safety skills
B-SS 9.	Demonstrate social maturity and behaviors appropriate to the situation and environment
B-SMS 10.	Demonstrate ability to manage transitions and ability to adapt to changing situations and responsibilities

GIRL WORLD

Session One: Finding Commonalities

Topic Overview

The group member will:

» Make introductions with other group members

» Identify the purpose of the group

» Discuss group rules/norms

» Identify some commonalities with other group members

Materials

» Reproducible: *Stand Up for Y-O-U!*

» Pencils

» Your selected items from the Appendix in the digital files

Procedures

Reminder – These session procedures will take about 1 hour to complete, so feel free to shorten or lengthen the session according to your time constraints. For ideas on how to do this, see the Recommendations for Starting a Counseling Group located at the beginning of this book. Of course, the more experienced you are with facilitating groups and with using this group curriculum, the more efficiently and quickly you will be able to guide group members through the procedures below.

1. Take attendance on the Group Notes sheet (included in Appendix).

2. Ask group members what they think they will learn about in this group and guide them to the idea that the purpose of the group is to support each other to become strong leaders, to build friendships, and to calmly handle interpersonal conflicts. Show the rules poster (included in Appendix), and have each group member read a rule aloud and share what she thinks the rule means. Remember to always remind group members that they can say "pass" if they do not want to read aloud.

3. Have each group member introduce herself by stating her name and something she's looking forward to. The group leader should go first to model this for group members.

4. Hand out the pretest (included in Appendix), and read aloud as group members fill in Yes/No for each statement. Collect and save these pretests until the last group session.

5. Tell the group that they will do an activity called *Stand Up for Y-O-U!* Read the series of statements on the *Stand Up for Y-O-U!* sheet to the group members. If they agree with the statement, they should stand. If they disagree, they should stay seated. The group leader can model this first with the first two statements in order to clarify directions. After all the statements have been read, discuss the *Stand Up for Y-O-U!* questions with the group.

6. Optional Homework Activity: Tell group members the following, "As you are hanging out with your friends over the next week, notice what qualities they have in common. For example, when I think of my friends, I notice that most of them are outgoing and funny, so those are two qualities that most of my friends have in common. We will talk about this next session."

7. Complete the group evaluation (included in Appendix). To do this, the group leader reads each evaluation statement aloud, and group members hold up fingers to indicate whether they agree/disagree/feel "sort of" about each statement. The group leader tallies group members' responses in each Agree/Sort of/Disagree column on the Group Notes sheet (included in Appendix) for use in planning the next session.

8. Sometimes this initial session can run a bit short, especially if the girls are feeling shy as new group members and if conversation is sparse. If you have extra time, the Friendship Collage from the Additional Activities (included in Appendix) is a wonderful way to wrap up this session.

Supplemental Forms and Handouts for Session One
(In Appendix in the digital files)
» Parent Permission Letter
» Group Notes
» Group Evaluation
» Pre/Post Test
» Group Rules & Consequences
» Group Pass Examples
» Data Analysis
» Additional Activities

Discussion Questions
» How did you feel while doing the Stand Up for Y-O-U activity? What did you like most and least about the activity? Explain.

» What are you most excited about learning or doing in this group? Explain.

» What are you most nervous about learning or doing in this group? Explain.

Stand Up for Y-O-U!

In this activity, group members should stand up when they agree with the statements below and sit down when they don't agree with them.

My favorite color is green.

I have a pet.

I have traveled outside of the state we live in.

I hate math.

I have no brothers or sisters.

I have heard a rumor or gossip about me before.

I have a best friend.

Someone has betrayed my trust.

I think it's okay for tweens to date.

I know someone who thinks about suicide.

I know someone who has been a victim of child abuse.

I have had a secret crush on someone.

I am excited about being a part of this group.

I like school.

I have traveled on an airplane.

I love math.

I have a sister

My parents are divorced.

I love pizza.

I have ended a friendship.

Sometimes I get really jealous.

I think I am a leader.

I worry about my weight.

I like the way I look.

I made a new friend this year.

I have seen something mean about me on the Internet, a computer, or a smartphone.

Someone in my family drinks alcohol too much or uses drugs.

{Discussion Questions}

1. What question did you like the best?
2. What question did you like the least?
3. Did any questions make you uncomfortable? Why?
4. Were you surprised by others' answers? Why?
5. Do you feel like you have some things in common with the girls of this group?
6. What were some of the questions where most of us stood up?
7. What did you like best and least about this activity?

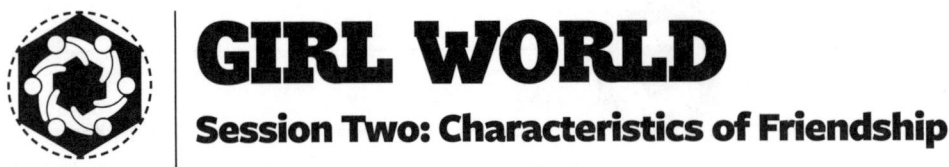

GIRL WORLD
Session Two: Characteristics of Friendship

Topic Overview

The group member will:

» Preview and make a prediction about a book on girl issues and/or empowerment

» Identify the qualities of good friendships

» Role-play how to start a conversation with a person you don't know

» Explore some strategies for ending a friendship

Materials

» Reproducibles: *Girl Empowerment-Themed Books to Use in Sessions, Friendship Role-play Cards*

» Read Aloud Book, Scrap Paper, Pencils, Chart Paper, Markers or Crayons

» Your selected items from the Appendix in the digital files

Procedures

1. Take attendance on the Group Notes sheet (included in Appendix). Ask group members whether there is anything they want to discuss relating to girl issues; guide them to limit responses/discussions to 5–10 minutes (see the recommendations section for tips on keeping within these time constraints).

2. Show the rules poster (included in Appendix), and have each group member read a rule aloud. Remember to always remind group members that they can say "pass" if they do not want to read aloud.

3. Show the read-aloud book and ask group members to guess what it might be about and make a prediction about what will happen in the book. Read some of the story aloud to group members and discuss some of the questions in *Girl Empowerment-Themed Books to Use in Sessions,* if there is time.

4. Ask group members to share what common qualities they noticed in their friends over the last week. Discuss that many of these qualities, if not all, are positive. Foster a discussion about the characteristics of positive friendships by asking group members to think for 30 seconds about what qualities they find most important in a friend/friendship. Write their ideas on chart paper. Summarize by starring the positive characteristics and reminding members that the starred characteristics are what they should have in their friendships, rather than any negative characteristics that might be on the chart.

5. Ask group members how they would start a conversation or friendship with a new person or group. Review the common practices of this with the group: introducing oneself, asking the new person his or her name and a question, inviting the new person to sit together or do a school activity together, etc. Then have each group member pick one of the *Friendship Role-play Cards*. The group leader models this first by picking and reading aloud a role-play card. With another group member acting as the "unknown" person/group, the group leader can model how to act out the role-play card showing a way to meet a new person. After the group leader models his/her card first with a volunteer, each group member can act out her role-play card, with the group leader playing the role of the "unknown" or new person(s). Depending on the comfort level and maturity of the group, you might allow each member to pick another group member to act out the new-girl role.

6. Discuss that knowing how to end a friendship is important too. On scrap paper, invite group members to take 5 minutes to draw how they might feel when a friendship ends. Allow members to share their drawings and ask group members to give some ideas on how they would end a friendship. Show the following questions and foster a brief discussion of each question, guiding them to the italicized ideas.

   » Who has had to end a friendship before? Why did you have to end the friendship? How did you end it?

   » When you have to end a friendship in the future, would you rather tell your friend you are ending the friendship, or would you just slowly start spending less time with her without having a conversation about it? Why? *Either is fine as long as you are polite, firm, and do what feels right to you.*

   » What is a toxic or unhealthy friendship? *A toxic or unhealthy relationship occurs when your "friend" puts you down, is jealous of your other friends, wants to change you, takes more than she gives, or won't ever do the activities you suggest.*

Supplemental Forms and Handouts for Session Two

(In Appendix in the digital files)
» Group Notes Sheet
» Group Rules & Consequences
» Group Evaluation
» Group Pass Examples
» Data Analysis
» Additional Activities

   » What does it mean to keep control and have boundaries in your friendships? *Don't let a friend tell you how to act or think, be friends with who you chose to be friends with, speak your thoughts and opinions politely, tell someone if they are upsetting you or if you need them to change their behavior towards you.*

   » How do you teach people how to treat you? Is this important? Why or why not? *This is very important because some people will treat you badly if you let them. Use your words (example- "I" messages) and keep good boundaries to show others how they should treat you- with consideration and respect! Believe in yourself!*

   » What should you do if you don't know if your friendship is toxic? *Talk to your parents, relatives, teachers, coaches, counselor, or another adult to get a second opinion.*

   *Alternately, if the language of some of these questions is too advanced for your group, you might try identifying key vocabulary before having the discussion (such as "toxic" and "boundaries," etc....), or you can skip the more challenging questions and just chart the ending-a-friendship ideas that your group members generate from the first 2 questions.

7. Optional Homework Activity: Ask group members to try out their new friendship skills by finding a new student at school and start up a conversation, if possible. Tell them you will talk about this during the next session.

8. Complete the group evaluation (included in Appendix). To do this, the group leader reads each evaluation statement aloud, and group members hold up fingers to indicate whether they agree/ disagree/feel "sort of" about each statement. The group leader tallies group members' responses in each Agree/Sort of/Disagree column on the Group Notes sheet (included in Appendix) for use in planning the next session.

Discussion Questions

» What was your best experience of making a new friend? Why was this the best one?

» What was the most surprising thing you learned today about ending friendships? Explain.

» What group rule is most important in your opinion? Why?

Books to Use in Sessions

Below is a list of excellent books that include themes of girl empowerment and handling girl issues. Also included are some examples of thought-provoking discussion questions in case you have extra time in your session and would like to explore the book's themes together through discussion. Since you will only have a short period of time to read aloud in each session, you may need to read only selected parts if you choose a chapter book or a lengthy picture book.

Possible Read-Aloud Titles

Just Josefina, by Valerie Tripp

13, by James Howe

Vicious, by Youth Communication

Hugging the Rock, by Susan Taylor Brown

Please Stop Laughing at Me, by Jodee Blanco

Speak, by Laurie Halse Anderson

Never Girls: In a Blink, by Kiki Thorpe

It's Not Drama, It's My Life, by Karin Kasdin

Josefina's Song, by Valerie Tripp

The Drama Years, by Haley Kirkpatrick

Girls to the Rescue #1, by Bruce Lansky

Thanks to Josefina, by Valerie Tripp

Stargirl, by Jerry Spinelli

Cut, by Patricia McCormick

Ladybug Girl, by David Soman

She Said What About Me? by Karen Dean

Letters to a Bullied Girl, by Olivia Gardner

Oops! The Manner Guide for Girls, by Nancy Holyoke

Dear Bully: Seventy Authors Tell Their Stories, by Megan Kelley Hall

Examples of Discussion Questions

1. What was your favorite part of the story? Why?
2. What was your least favorite part of the story? Why?
3. Who is an important character in this story?
4. Describe the location of the story.
5. What is the most exciting event?
6. What is the saddest event?
7. What did you learn from the story?
8. Where does the character work or go in the story?
9. Do you know anyone who has been bullied? How do you feel about this?
10. How many family members/siblings does the character have?
11. What did the character say?
12. What is the problem in the story? Tell me about a problem in your life.
13. What is the solution? What kinds of solutions do you like?
14. Does anyone in the story change? Tell me about someone you know who changed.
15. Why is the character [*insert emotion word*]? Do you ever feel [*same emotion word*]?

Friendship Role-play Cards

1. Cut out the friendship role-play cards in the chart below and put them in a decorated box.

2. Have each group member take one role-play card from the box.

3. The group leader picks a volunteer to be the new/unknown person in a role-playing scenario, and then the group leader models how to use the role-play card to act out meeting a new or unknown person/group (group member volunteer) by introducing herself, asking the unknown person her name, asking a question, and extending an invitation.

4. With the group leader acting as the unknown person/group, the group member acts out the role-play card by:
   » Introducing herself
   » Asking the unknown person's name
   » Asking the unknown person a question (Where are you from? What kind of movies/books/music do you like?, etc.)
   » Extending an invitation to the unknown person (to sit together at lunch, do a school activity, etc.)

For role-playing scenarios requiring a group, the group leader can ask for multiple volunteers to act as unknown people.

The counselor just brought a new girl into your classroom. The teacher seats her next to you and you'd like to get to know her.	Three girls are chatting about movies in the school bathroom. You'd like to talk to them. How do you start the conversation?
A new person is sitting alone at lunch. You'd like to invite her to your table to eat.	A girl you've never met before is an amazing artist in your art class. You want to talk to her about her art and get to know her.
The new girl in your class just moved here from Houston, Texas, where you used to live! How will you talk to her about this?	You really want to sit at the lunch table of a group of girls who seem really nice. You'd like to get to know them. How do you make this happen?
A group of four friends in your after-school club seem really fun and cool. You'd like to hang out with them. How do you introduce yourself to them?	In PE, the new student doesn't have anyone to be her tennis partner. How can you help her out and get to know her better (which you have been wanting to do)?
After school breakfast, a new student seems lost. Your best friend moved away last year, so you are looking for a new friend. How do you help the student and get to know her?	A person you don't know starts talking to you on the bus. She wants to know where kids hang out most. She seems really cool and you'd like to hang out with her.

GIRL WORLD
Session Three: Handling Relational Aggression & Cyberbullying

Topic Overview

The group member will:

» Continue reading the book on girl empowerment to identify ways girls resolve conflicts, strengthen relationships, and cope in healthful ways

» Define and give examples of relational aggression

» Identify strategies to avoid cyberbullying

» Make a sign showing others how to avoid or handle cyberbullying

Materials

» Reproducibles: *Girl Empowerment-Themed Books to Use in Sessions* (from last session), *Relational Aggression Cards, Strategies to Avoid Cyberbullying*

» A Read-Aloud Book

» Various art materials for cyberbullying signs such as pencils, markers, crayons, chart or poster paper, magazine clippings, glue, and scissors

» Your selected items from the Appendix in the digital files

Procedures

1. Take attendance on the Group Notes sheet (included in Appendix). Read some of the story aloud to group members and discuss some of the questions in *Girl Empowerment-Themed Books to Use in Sessions* (from last session), if there is time. Ask them whether there is anything they want to discuss relating to girl issues; guide them to limit responses/discussions to 5–10 minutes (see the recommendations section for tips on keeping within these time constraints).

2. Show the rules poster (included in Appendix), and have each group member read a rule aloud. Remember to always remind group members that they can say "pass" if they do not want to read aloud.

3. Ask group members to share any experiences they had with making a new friend or meeting someone new over the past week.

4. Ask group members to take some guesses at the meaning of the term "relational aggression." Discuss that it occurs when someone uses relationships to hurt or bully another person. Now is also a good time to review the definition of bullying: when someone who has more power than another hurts that person on purpose repeatedly by using his or her superior power or position.

5. Have each group member chose one of the *Relational Aggression Cards*, read it aloud, and then discuss a time when she experienced it or saw someone else experience it.

6. Ask group members how relational aggression occurs on the Internet, smartphones, social media, or computers. Discuss that this is called cyberbullying and then hand out the *Strategies to Avoid Cyberbullying* sheet. Read the strategies together in round-robin style.

7. Tell group members that they will each be making a sign to show others how to avoid or handle cyberbullying. Make various art materials available to the group, such as markers, crayons, chart or poster paper, magazine clippings, glue, scissors, etc. It is a good idea to show group members an example of the cyberbullying avoidance sign first so they will have an idea of what they are creating. Group members should choose their favorite strategy from *Strategies to Avoid Cyberbullying* and create a sign with a title, picture, and the strategy sentence to inform their peers about cyberbullying. Decide as a group how to display the signs.

8. Optional Homework Activity: Ask group members to be on the lookout between now and next session for examples of relational aggression. Tell them you will talk about this during the next session.

9. Complete the group evaluation (included in Appendix). To do this, the group leader reads each evaluation statement aloud, and group members hold up fingers to indicate whether they agree/disagree/feel "sort of" about each statement. The group leader tallies group members' responses in each Agree/Sort of/ Disagree column on the Group Notes sheet (included in Appendix) for use in planning the next session.

Supplemental Forms and Handouts for Session Three

(In Appendix in the digital files)
» Group Notes Sheet
» Group Rules & Consequences
» Group Evaluation
» Group Pass Examples
» Data Analysis
» Additional Activities

Discussion Questions

» What advice would you give a girl who is struggling with relational aggression or cyberbullying?

» How did you feel during the relational aggression card activity? Explain how you found it helpful or unhelpful.

» What was the best part of making your cyberbullying sign? Explain.

Relational Aggression Cards

Directions: Cut up these cards and put them in a jar to use in sessions three and six.

Laughing and Pointing	Ignoring Someone	Making Mean Jokes
Spreading Rumors	Texting Hurtful Messages	Excluding Someone From the Group
Imitating Someone In A Mean Way	Rolling Eyes	Embarrassing Someone on Purpose
Giving Someone A Mean Look	Gossiping about Someone	Telling Others Not to be Friends with Someone
Writing Mean Things about Someone on Social Media	Posting Embarrassing Photos of Someone on Social Media	Huddling Together and Whispering about Others
Backstabbing	Using Code Names to Talk about Others	Telling an Ex-friend's Secrets
Talking Badly about Others	Passing Mean Notes to Someone In Class	

Strategies to Avoid Cyberbullying

Refuse to pass along cyberbullying messages.

Tell friends to stop cyberbullying.

Block communication with cyberbullies
(unfriend them on social media, etc.)

Report cyberbullying to a trusted adult.

Report social media cyberbullying to the website.

Never post or share your personal information online
(this includes your full name, address, telephone number, school
name, parents' names, credit card number, or social security
number) or your friends' personal information.

Never share your Internet passwords with anyone, except
your parents or guardians.

Never meet anyone face-to-face whom you only know online.

Talk to your parents/guardians about what you do online.

Only accept online requests (like friend requests) from
people you know.

Never post something you wouldn't want your family, teachers,
or future employer to see.

Don't pretend to be someone you're not.

Review your privacy settings often and set them so that only
friends and family can see you online.

GIRL WORLD

Session Four: Finding Solutions for Rumors and Gossip

Topic Overview

The group member will:

» Continue reading the book on girl empowerment to identify ways girls resolve conflicts, strengthen relationships, and cope in healthful ways

» Define and give examples of rumors/gossip causing conflict

» Identify and role-play strategies to handle rumors/gossip in healthful ways

Materials

» Reproducibles: *Rumors and Gossip, Girl Empowerment-Themed Books to Use in Sessions* (from session two)

» A Read-Aloud Book, Chart Paper, Markers

» Your selected items from the Appendix in the digital files

Procedures

1. Take attendance on the Group Notes sheet (included in Appendix). Read some of the story aloud to group members and discuss some of the questions in *Girl Empowerment-Themed Books to Use in Sessions* (from session two), if there is time. Ask them whether there is anything they want to discuss relating to girl issues; guide them to limit responses/discussions to 5–10 minutes (see the recommendations section for tips on keeping within these time constraints).

2. Show the rules poster (included in Appendix), and have each group member read a rule aloud. Remember to always remind group members that they can say "pass" if they do not want to read aloud.

3. Ask group members to share any times during the past week when they witnessed an example of relational aggression. Briefly brainstorm some ways that the victim of the relational aggression situation might have been helped to feel better.

4. Read the rumor conflict aloud from the *Rumors and Gossip* sheet and then have group members brainstorm healthful ways to handle rumors.

5. Show the group the Rumor/Gossip Solutions from the *Rumors and Gossip* sheet; consider writing the solutions on chart paper for more emphasis. Working in round-robin style, have group members read each solution and briefly discuss the meaning of each one.

6. Model for group members how to role-play a favorite rumor/gossip solution from the *Rumors and Gossip* sheet or chart paper. Describe a typical but simple rumor/gossip problem at the school, and then ask for a volunteer to act out her favorite rumor/gossip solution while the group leader tries to involve the volunteer in talking about the rumor/gossip. After the modeling, give each group member a chance to role-play her favorite rumor/gossip solution while the group leader tries to involve her in the rumor/gossip. You might even have the group suggest different rumor scenarios for members to role-play with the group leader.

7. Optional Homework Activity: Ask group members to use one of the rumor/gossip solutions over the next week to handle a rumor or gossip situation. Tell them that they will share their experiences with this during the next session.

8. Complete the group evaluation (included in Appendix). To do this, the group leader reads each evaluation statement aloud, and group members hold up fingers to indicate whether they agree/disagree/feel "sort of" about each statement. The group leader tallies group members' responses in each Agree/Sort of/Disagree column on the Group Notes sheet (included in Appendix) for use in planning the next session.

Supplemental Forms and Handouts for Session Four

(In Appendix in the digital files)

» Group Notes Sheet

» Group Evaluation

» Group Rules & Consequences

» Group Pass Examples

» Data Analysis

» Additional Activities

Discussion Questions

» When was a time in your life that a rumor really hurt you or a friend of yours? What made this experience so hurtful?

» What is your favorite way to solve a rumor? Why is it your favorite?

» Do you think a rumor or gossip could actually harm someone's health? If so, how?

Rumors & Gossip

Rumor Conflict

Sarah and Jessica have been friends since 7th grade. They know all of each other's secrets. Then, last week Brian asked Sarah to be his girlfriend and Jessica got mad when Sarah said yes because Jessica had a crush on him first! Now, Jessica is spreading rumors that Sarah stole Brian from her, and all the 10th graders are talking about this and giving Sarah mean looks or ignoring her.

What would you do if you were:

a. Sarah

_____

_____

_____

b. A Student at this School

_____

_____

_____

Rumor/Gossip Solutions

» Change the subject.

» Walk away.

» Use an "I" message. For example, "I don't want to gossip. Please leave me out of it."

» Laugh and say it's ridiculous.

» Tell the person it's none of their business.

» Ask the person if you should refer them to the counselor for support.

» Say something nice about the person instead.

GIRL WORLD
Session Five: Are Your Coping Skills Healthy?

Topic Overview

The group member will:

» Continue reading the book on girl empowerment to identify ways girls resolve conflicts, strengthen relationships, and cope in healthful ways

» Identify and compare healthy and unhealthy coping skills

» Choose her favorite healthy coping skill

Materials

» Reproducibles: *Coping Skills Letter, Healthy Coping Skills, Coping Skills Bingo, Girl Empowerment-Themed Books to Use in Sessions* (from session two)

» Pencils, A Read-Aloud Book, Items to use as Bingo Chips

» Your selected items from the Appendix in the digital files

Procedures

1. Take attendance on the Group Notes sheet (included in Appendix). Read some of the story aloud to group members and discuss some of the questions in *Girl Empowerment-Themed Books to Use in Sessions* (from session two), if there is time. Ask them whether there is anything they want to discuss relating to girl issues; guide them to limit responses/discussions to 5–10 minutes (see the recommendations section for tips on keeping within these time constraints).

2. Show the rules poster (included in Appendix), and have each group member read a rule aloud. Remember to always remind group members that they can say "pass" if they do not want to read aloud.

3. Ask group members to share their experiences over the past week with handling a rumor or gossip using their rumor/gossip solution from last session.

4. Discuss with group members the definition of coping skills from *Coping Skills Letter*, and briefly discuss the difference between healthy versus unhealthy coping skills.

5. Read the *Need Coping Help* letter to the group, and ask group members what advice they would give the writer. Read group members the Girl World response to *Need Coping Help* and then hand out the *Healthy Coping Skills* sheet.

6. Have group members read the *Healthy Coping Skills* list in a round-robin fashion. Give a brief explanation of each skill and have each group member circle her favorite one.

7. Brainstorm ways for group members to remember to use their circled coping skills during difficult times, such as: keep it on the bedside table to read each night before bed, post it on the bathroom mirror to read each morning while brushing their teeth, or put it in their smartphone as a daily reminder. Have each group member share how she will remember to use her favorite coping skill. If there is time, discuss the questions in the *Healthy Coping Skills* sheet.

8. Hand out a *Coping Skills Bingo* template to each group member. Have group members copy the bolded healthy coping skills words from their Healthy Coping Skills sheet onto the Bingo template in any random order. Play Coping Skills Bingo. It is a good idea to play this in future sessions during the last 5–10 minutes of group so that group members keep the coping skills fresh in their minds.

9. Optional Homework Activity: Ask group members to use their favorite coping skill between now and the next session when they have a painful thought or memory. Tell them that they will share their experiences with using the coping skills during the next session.

10. Complete the group evaluation (included in Appendix). To do this, the group leader reads each evaluation statement aloud, and group members hold up fingers to indicate whether they agree/ disagree/feel "sort of" about each statement. The group leader tallies group members' responses in each Agree/Sort of/Disagree column on the Group Notes sheet (included in Appendix) for use in planning the next session.

Discussion Questions

» Do you know someone who uses unhealthy coping skills? What do you think of this?

» How do you think people might have problems if they use an unhealthy coping skill?

» Did you like or dislike playing *Coping Skills Bingo?* Why or why not?

» Describe some of your favorite ways to cope.

Supplemental Forms and Handouts for Session Five
(In Appendix in the digital files)

» Group Notes Sheet

» Group Evaluation

» Group Rules & Consequences

» Group Pass Examples

» Data Analysis

» Additional Activities

Coping Skills Letter

Definition

Coping skills are the ways that we handle difficult moments in our lives such as a bad memory, getting in trouble, failing a test, a relationship breakup, etc.

A Few Examples of Healthy Versus Unhealthy Coping Skills

Healthy	Unhealthy
» Vent to a friend	» Yell at someone
» Take a walk	» Fight
» Write in your journal	» Take drugs

Need Coping Help Letter and Response

Dear Girl World,

I have had a lot of bad things happen in my life, like my parents getting divorced when I was in 5th grade and losing most of my friends in middle school. So, I have a lot of stress and painful thoughts and I need to know what things can help me cope with this. I have been feeling really sad and angry lately, so I'd like to know if there are any good ways to deal with my awful memories and painful thoughts that I have.

Signed,

Need Coping Help

Dear Need Coping Help,

We are really sorry that you are feeling so bad lately, but remember that all bad feelings pass eventually. In the meantime, there are lots of healthy coping skills to help you get through this rough time and deal with your painful thoughts and memories. Take a look at them and circle your favorite one on the *Healthy Coping Skills* handout. Then review your favorite coping skill everyday so you remember to use it.

Good Luck,

Girl World

Healthy Coping Skills

Vent to a friend/family member.

Exercise.

Write your feelings in a **journal**.

Make a **plan** for how to solve/handle what's bothering you.

Look for the **positive** in your situation.

Be creative: Draw! Paint! Sing! Act!

Substitute a good behavior for the one that is bothering you.

Meditate or do **relaxation** exercises.

Spend time with your **pet**(s).

Talk to a **counselor, doctor** or other adult.

Eat well and **sleep** well.

Discussion Questions

Which healthy coping skills above are unclear to you?

Circle your favorite coping skill. Why is it your favorite?

What is an example of an unhealthy coping skill?
What makes it unhealthy?

Role-play one of the coping skills above with a partner.

Coping Skills Bingo

Hand out blank Bingo cards and have group members fill in the bolded healthy coping skills words in any mixed-up order on their card. Group members can use beans or pebbles as game pieces. First, call out a Bingo letter and coping skill. Second, repeat the Bingo letter and coping skill. The first group member to get five beans/pebbles placed in a row or column calls out "BINGO" and wins a prize. After someone wins, have group members clear their cards of game pieces and start again. Collect the Bingo cards after the game to be handed out again for a future game.

B	I	N	G	O
		FREE SPACE ☺		

GIRL WORLD
Session Six: Solving Conflicts the Peaceful Way

Topic Overview

The group member will:

» Continue reading the book on girl empowerment to identify ways girls resolve conflicts, strengthen relationships, and cope in healthful ways

» Use "I" messages to communicate feelings and needs in a nonthreatening way

» Use the four steps of conflict resolution to solve an interpersonal problem

Materials

» Reproducibles; *The Four Steps of Conflict Resolution, Healthy Coping Skills* (from last session), *Girl Empowerment-Themed Books to Use in Sessions* (from session two)

» Pencils, Chart Paper, Markers, A Read-Aloud Book, Jar or Container for the *Relational Aggression Cards* (from session three)

» Your selected items from the Appendix in the digital files

Procedures

1. Take attendance on the Group Notes sheet (included in Appendix). Read some of the story aloud to group members and discuss some of the questions in *Girl Empowerment-Themed Books to Use in Sessions* (from session two), if there is time. Ask them whether there is anything they want to discuss relating to girl issues; guide them to limit responses/discussions to 5–10 minutes (see the recommendations section for tips on keeping within this time constraint).

2. Show the rules poster (included in Appendix), and have each group member read a rule aloud Remember to always remind group members that they can say "pass" if they do not want to read aloud.

3. Review the *Healthy Coping Skills* list (from last session) with group members and have each member tell again their favorite coping skill. Ask members to share a time during the past week when they used their coping skill to deal with a painful thought or memory.

4. Show the *Four Steps to Conflict Resolution* on chart paper and discuss each step. Ask group members how they have already used these steps in their lives. The group leader should model each of the steps for the group while a volunteer kicks the group leader's chair as the "bothering" action. Discuss how steps one through three should only be used in minor conflicts; tell group members that anytime someone threatens them or puts their hands on them, they should go straight to step four.

5. Role-play each conflict resolution step with group members. Have a group member pick a *Relational Aggression Card* (from session three) from the jar and read the card to the group leader, who will then act out the card behavior in order to "bother" that group member. In this way, the group member can practice using each of the four steps to deal with the bothering person. Repeat with each group member.

6. Optional Homework Activity: Ask group members to practice using the four conflict resolution steps between now and the next session whenever they have an interpersonal conflict. Briefly brainstorm some conflicts that are interpersonal (for example, an argument with a friend) and some conflicts that are not interpersonal (for example, falling off your bike or board). Tell group members that they will share their experiences with the four conflict resolution steps at the beginning of the next session.

7. Complete the group evaluation (included in Appendix). To do this, the group leader reads each evaluation statement aloud, and group members hold up fingers to indicate whether they agree/disagree/feel "sort of" about each statement. The group leader tallies group members' responses in each Agree/Sort of/Disagree column on the Group Notes (included in Appendix) for use in planning the next session.

Discussion Questions

» How did you feel while role-playing the Four Steps of Conflict Resolution? Explain.

» In your opinion, what is the most important thing that you have learned in group so far? Why is this important to you?

» How will you be able to use this important knowledge that you've learned in group in your future?

Supplemental Forms and Handouts for Session Six

(In Appendix in the digital files)
» Group Notes Sheet
» Group Evaluation
» Group Rules & Consequences
» Group Pass Examples
» Data Analysis
» Additional Activities

The Four Steps to Conflict Resolution

{ One }
Ignore.

{ Two }
Walk Away.

{ Three }
Say an "I" Message.

For example:
I don't like it when you yell at me, so please stop.

I don't like it when you write mean things about me on Facebook, so don't do it again.

I feel annoyed when you touch my desk, so stop touching it.

{ Four }
Tell an adult who can help you solve the conflict.

GIRL WORLD
Session Seven: What to do When Romance is in the Air!

Topic Overview

The group member will:

» Continue reading the book on girl empowerment to identify ways girls resolve conflicts, strengthen relationships, and cope in healthful ways

» Identify characteristics and behaviors of healthy romantic relationships

» Discuss group members' feelings about romantic relationships

» Create acrostic artwork to show characteristics of healthy dating

Materials

» Reproducibles: *Dating Dos and Don'ts, The Four Steps of Conflict Resolution* (from last session), *Girl Empowerment-Themed Books to Use in Sessions* (from session two), *Coping Skills Bingo* (from session five)

» A Read-Aloud Book, Chart Paper, Items for Bingo chips, Various Art Materials for Acrostic Artwork (pencils, markers, crayons, paper, magazine clippings, glue, and scissors)

» Your selected items from the Appendix in the digital files

Procedures

1. Take attendance on the Group Notes sheet (included in Appendix). Read some of the story aloud to group members and discuss some of the questions in *Girl Empowerment-Themed Books to Use in Sessions* (from session two), if there is time. Ask them whether there is anything they want to discuss relating to girl issues; guide them to limit responses/discussions to 5–10 minutes (see the recommendations section for tips on keeping within this time constraint). Discuss with the group that the next session will be the last scheduled session. Tell the group members they can meet with you individually on an as-needed basis and give them the procedures for requesting this. In addition, ask them whether they would like a follow-up group session in one month and if so, schedule it. See the recommendations section at the beginning of this guide for tips and content of the follow-up session.

2. Show the rules poster (included in Appendix), and have each group member read a rule aloud. Remember to always remind group members that they can say "pass" if they do not want to read aloud.

3. Have group members share their experiences with using *the Four Steps to Conflict Resolution* (from last session) during the previous week when they had an interpersonal problem.

   » If you feel your group members are too young to discuss the dating topic, feel free to skip procedures #4-6 and substitute one of the Additional Activities (included in Appendix) instead.

4   Ask group members, "At what age is it good to start dating?" Guide group members to the realization that older is always better for starting to date and that the age to start dating is a decision they should make with their parents/guardians.

5. Show *Dating Dos and Don'ts* on chart paper. Have group members read each bullet point in round-robin style, then lead a discussion of the dating questions on *Dating Dos and Don'ts*.

6. Have group members create their own acrostic artwork of healthy dating habits by writing the word DATING on paper in a vertical column. Then have members use each letter of DATING to start a phrase about healthy relationship habits (refer to Dating Do's & Don'ts for ideas). For example, "D" could be used for *do stay positive*, "A" could be used for *act like you normally do*, and "N" could be used for *never put yourself down*, etc. Once group members have finished writing the healthy habits, they can illustrate each one in various pictures around the acrostic. Make art materials available to the group, such as markers, crayons, chart or poster paper, magazine clippings, glue, scissors, etc. It is a good idea to show group members an example of this acrostic art first so they will have an idea of what they are creating. Finally, collect the artwork and display in the group counseling room.

> ### Supplemental Forms and Handouts for Session Seven
> (In Appendix in the digital files)
> » Group Notes Sheet
> » Group Evaluation
> » Group Rules & Consequences
> » Group Pass Examples
> » Data Analysis
> » Additional Activities

7. If there is time, play *Coping Skills Bingo* (from session five) to review coping skills with group members.

8. Optional Homework Activity: Ask group members to start the dating conversation with their parents/guardians by asking them the question, "At what age is it good to start dating?" If group members are comfortable, they can share some of the bullet points from *Dating Dos and Don'ts* with their parents/guardians to continue the discussion. If a group member is too uncomfortable to ask her parents/guardians the dating age question, suggest that she write down the age question in a note to her parents/guardians, telling them that she feels uncomfortable talking about this topic and asking them to write her back; she should then leave the note in a place where her parents/guardians will see it. Tell group members that they will share their experiences during the next session.

9. Complete the group evaluation (included in Appendix). To do this, the group leader reads each evaluation statement aloud, and group members hold up fingers to indicate whether they agree/disagree/feel "sort of" about each statement. The group leader tallies group members' responses in each Agree/Sort of/Disagree column on the Group Notes sheet (included in Appendix) for use in planning the next session.

Discussion Questions

» How do you feel about talking to your parents/guardians about dating? Explain.

» What have you learned about others in our group?

» How are you feeling about group ending next session? Explain.

Dating Do's & Don'ts

Dating is an important part of growing up that shouldn't be started prematurely. It takes a lot of maturity to date healthfully without intense painful feelings. That's why the saying, "the older, the better" definitely applies to the age at which you should start dating. Another important part of the decision about when to start dating involves your parents/guardians; the right age for you to start dating is the age that your parents/guardians determine with you. Below are some tips for healthful dating and then some questions about dating.

DO: Be Yourself and Be Safe

DO talk about things you have in common.

DO act like you normally do.

DO say nice things about yourself, your crush, and others.

DO wear neat, well-fitting clothes.

DO stay positive!

DON'T: Be Unsafe or Be Mean

DON'T lie about your age.

DON'T drink, smoke, or take drugs to look cool.

DON'T wear tight or revealing clothes to get attention.

DON'T gossip or talk negatively about others to get attention.

DON'T put yourself down.

Dating Questions

What is more important: to have good friendships or to have a romantic relationship? Why?

What do you think of girls who aren't dating yet? Is there something wrong with them? Are they waiting until they are ready?

Is it fine to be more interested in romantic relationships than friendships? Why or why not?

Why don't all girls start dating at the same age?

In your opinion, what is the most important quality in a romantic relationship? A friendship? Why?

GIRL WORLD
Session Eight: Reflections and Body Image

Topic Overview

The group member will:

» Finish reading the book on girl empowerment to identify ways girls resolve conflicts, strengthen relationships, and cope in healthful ways

» Reflect on her learnings/experiences with the group

» Evaluate the group experience

» Analyze the media's portrayal of women and girls in unhealthy and unnatural ways

Materials

» Reproducibles: *Group Experience Evaluation, Body Image & the Media, Girl Empowerment-Themed Books to Use in Sessions* (from session two), *Coping Skills Bingo* (from session five), *Pre/Posttests* (from session one)

» A Read-Aloud Book, Chart Paper, Markers, Pencils, Items to use as Bingo chips, and access to the Internet and Technology (such as a laptop)

» Your selected items from the Appendix in the digital files

Procedures

1. Take attendance on the Group Notes sheet (included in Appendix). Finish the read-aloud book. If time allows, discuss some of the questions from *Girl Empowerment-Themed Books to Use in Sessions* (from session two), such as, "What did you learn from the story?" Ask group members whether there is anything they want to discuss relating to girl issues; guide them to limit responses/discussions to 5–10 minutes (see the recommendations section for tips on keeping within this time constraint). Remind the group that this is the last group session, and briefly discuss plans for the follow-up session, if you will be having one.

2. Show the rules poster (included in Appendix), and have each group member read a rule aloud, unless they say "pass."

3. Have group members share their experiences with talking to their parents/guardians about the dating question/s from the last session.

4. Review with group members all the main points learned during the Girl World sessions. To best facilitate this review, give group members 1 minute to think of the main things they learned in group and then write their responses on chart paper.

5. Hand out the *Pre/Posttest* (from session one) and read it aloud as group members fill in Yes/No for each posttest statement. Make sure group members write answers in the posttest column and don't change any of their pretest answers. Collect and save the completed posttests for data purposes.

6. Complete the *Group Experience Evaluation*. To do this, the group leader reads each evaluation statement aloud while group members write down their response to that statement. Collect and retain the completed evaluations for data purposes.

7. Ask group members whether the images they see of girls/women on TV, in movies, and in magazines are representative of the way these girls/women appear in real life. Guide members to the realization that experts on hair, makeup, and clothes spend hours on these girls/women before we see them on TV/in movies/in magazines. Then further explain to group members that other experts use computers and software to change the look of the girls'/women's bodies, faces, and hair.

Supplemental Forms and Handouts for Session Eight
(In Appendix in the digital files)

» Group Notes Sheet
» Group Evaluation
» Pre/Post Test
» Group Rules & Consequences
» Group Pass Examples
» Data Analysis
» Additional Activities

8. Do an Internet search to find photos of celebrities with and without media touchups (you can even use the search term *Photoshop Celebrities*). Show group members the Internet photos and follow the viewing with the discussion questions from *Body Image & the Media*.

9. If there is time, play *Coping Skills Bingo* (from session five) to review coping skills with group members.

10. Praise the group members for all of their hard work. Ask whether there is anything more they would like to discuss or any other help they need. Remind them to let you know if they need to meet with you anytime in the future.

Discussion Questions

» What session did you like the best? Why?

» Rate your feelings about group ending today on a scale of 1-10 with 1 being unhappy and 10 being happy. Explain your rating.

» What is your goal for yourself now that group is over? Why?

» Name two things you liked best about group.

» How would you like to continue to be supported by your counselor/leader and the counseling office in the future?

Body Image & the Media

Body Image Photos and Videos on the Internet

Do an Internet search to find photos of celebrities with and without media touchups (you can even use the search term *Photoshop Celebrities*). Show group members the Internet photos and follow the viewing with the discussion questions. Alternately, you can search the Internet a bit more thoroughly to find links to body image public service announcement (PSA) videos – Dove, Girl Scouts, and WatchWellcast are just a few of the organizations that provide these types of PSAs.

Discussion Questions after Viewing Photos

» What makes someone beautiful in your opinion? Do we all have the same opinion?

» Who creates the pictures of women/girls in the media?

» Who benefits from these pictures? How do they benefit?

» Why are girls sensitive to the media's body image ideal?

» Do you think boys feel pressure about body image? How?

» How do images we see in the media affect us?

» What kinds of things do girls do to look like the images in the media?

» How do the media images make you feel?

Group Experience Evaluation   Date: _____

Congratulations on completing this Girl World group program! Making changes in your life and setting goals for yourself is hard work, but the success you experience as a result of accomplishing goals feels awesome. Please take a few minutes now to reflect on what you've learned in group and then answer the following questions.

1. What have you learned about yourself through our group experience?

_____

_____

_____

2. How will these learnings affect you in the future?

_____

_____

_____

3. Would you recommend this group to a friend? Why or why not?

_____

_____

_____

4. Which group activity did you find most useful?

_____

_____

_____

5. Which group activity did you find least useful?

_____

_____

_____

6. What did you learn about other people during the group experience?

_____

_____

_____

7. Additional Comments:

_____

_____

_____

References

If you would like to learn more about any of the strategies or activities in this counseling guide, please refer to the sources below.

"ASCA Mindsets & Behaviors for Student Success: K-12 College- and Career-Readiness Standards for Every Student." Accessed November 22, 2016. https://schoolcounselor.org/asca/media/asca/home/MindsetsBehaviors.pdf.

American School Counselor Association. (2019). *The ASCA National Model 4th Ed.* Alexandria, VA: author.

Senn, Diane. *Bullying in the Girl's World: A School-Wide Approach to Girl Bullying.* Chapin, SC: Youthlight, 2007.

"Facebook for Educators and Community Leaders." Accessed March 1, 2014. http://fbhost.promotw.com/fbpages/img/safety_resources/ffeclg.pdf.

Gordon, Thomas. *Parent Effectiveness Training: The Proven Program for Raising Responsible Children.* 30th ed. Massachusetts: Harmony, 2000.

Kaffenberger, Carol. *Making Data Work.* 3rd ed. Alexandria, VA: American School Counselor Association, 2013.

Lerner, Stephanie. *Where There's a Goal, There's a Way: Individual Counseling Guide.* Elgin, TX: Bilingual Learner, 2013.

Sklare, Gerald. *Brief Counseling That Works: A Solution-Focused Approach for School Counselors and Administrators.* 2nd ed. Thousand Oaks, CA: Corwin, 2004.

Wellcast, http://www.watchwellcast.com/.

Girl World Appendix Forms (in the digital files)

- » Parent Permission Letter
- » Group Notes Sheet
- » Group Evaluation
- » Pre/Post Test
- » Group Rules & Consequences
- » Group Pass Examples
- » Data Analysis
- » Additional Activities

Parent Permission Letter

Date: _____

Dear Parent/Guardian:

The Comprehensive School Counseling Program at _____ School includes small group counseling sessions. Your child _____, has been referred for participation in one of these counseling groups. With your permission, your child will attend group counseling on a scheduled basis at school by the school counselor. These group sessions will focus on the topic of _____. The sessions will not change the child's academic program. Participation in the group is voluntary, and confidentiality will be discussed in group and respected.

At times, the school counselor and school-based staff (principal, assistant principal, social worker, psychologist, behavior specialist, teacher, nurse, etc.) will need to exchange information about your child (goals, strategies, etc.). All communication will take place only on an educational need-to-know basis.

This permission is for the school year _____.

If you would like for your child to have small group sessions with the school counselor, please sign and return this form to the counseling office.

If you have any questions or concerns, please call _____.

Thank you,

_____

School Counselor

I grant permission for _____ to participate in small group counseling sessions with the school counselor.

_____

Parent Signature

_____

Phone Number

Girl World Pre/Posttest

Name: _____ Date: _____

PRETEST: YES –OR– NO/I DON'T KNOW	Statements	POSTTEST: YES –OR– NO/I DON'T KNOW
	I can name three healthy coping skills.	
	I can give some examples of relational aggression.	
	If someone spreads rumors about me, I know how to stop him or her in a peaceful way.	
	I can name the four steps of conflict resolution.	
	I know how to start a conversation or game with a new person that I might want to be friends with.	

Group Rules & Consequences

{ Group Rules }

Only say helpful comments.

Don't tell others what is said in the group.

One person talks at a time; there are no side conversations.

Use the bathroom before or after group only.

Name-calling is not allowed.

Don't touch someone else's stuff.

If you arrive late, bring a pass with the time/an adult signature.

{ Consequences }

Private Warning

Removal from Group

Group Pass Examples

Get your lunch at 11:15 and bring it to the counselor's office to eat TODAY at 4th period.

Come to the counselor's office TODAY at 12:30.

Come to room 504 TODAY during PE. Please bring this pass.

Additional Activities

As mentioned in the recommendations section, these are additional activities for extending or replacing certain sessions.

Some parts of these additional activities may need modification for very young group members. If necessary, the group leader might read aloud while young group members follow along with their finger. In addition, young group members might dictate to the group leader when necessary (for example with the notecard goals) rather than writing on their own.

Friendship Collage

Start this activity by reviewing (or introducing, if necessary) the characteristics of positive friendships list that the group created in session two. Tell group members that they will make a group collage showing as many of these characteristics as they can. Provide a large piece of poster paper, markers, scissors, glue, and lots of magazines for group members to use in creating the group friendship collage. Before letting group members start the collage, it is best to model this activity by identifying a few magazine pictures that represent some of the positive friendship characteristics, then quickly cutting them out and gluing them on the poster as an example. Have the group members start their collage by agreeing on and designing the poster title.

Who's Afraid of the Green Monster?

If you haven't done session four with group members yet, define the word rumor with the group. Discuss with group members the link between jealousy and rumors (often they have a cause–effect relationship). Explain that jealousy is a normal, acceptable human emotion that everyone feels, but problems can occur when people handle their jealousy in unhealthful ways (like spreading rumors). Have the group brainstorm healthful ways to handle jealousy. Next have each group member illustrate a healthy way to manage her jealousy and an unhealthy way to manage jealousy. It is best to show the group an example of this art project so they have an idea of the final product. All members can then present their illustrations to the group.

Where There's a Goal, There's a Way

Start off this activity with the following Friendship Quiz. Hand out the quiz and read each statement aloud to the group while members circle their answer. Based on their "No" responses, read and discuss the corresponding good friend tips. Ask group members to create a goal for themselves based on a "No" response or based on something they'd like to achieve. Show the following prompt for group members to use as they write their goal on a notecard:

My goal is to _____.

The group leader should model this first, guiding group members to create a goal that is specific, realistic, and measurable—for example, my goal is to introduce myself to one new person next week. Finally, have each group member read her goal aloud to the group. In closing, the group leader should collect the notecards and photocopy them after group; give the originals back to group members as a reminder to practice their goals during the week. Keep photocopies so that group members can share successes with their goals in the next group session.

Friendship Quiz: Do You Have What It Takes to be a Good Friend?

YES   NO   When my friend starts to spend more time with a girl other than me, I stay calm and look for other girls with which to spend MY time.

YES   NO   When I want to make a new friend, I know how to gently introduce myself to her and ask whether she wants to talk or do something together.

YES   NO   I know how to gently and politely spend less time with one friend and more time with other girls.

YES   NO   I know the characteristics of a positive friendship.

YES   NO   I know how to keep a friend but still speak my own opinions and continue with my own habits.

YES   NO   I understand that different girls are comfortable with different things, and I accept my friends even when their ideas are different from mine.

YES   NO   I know how to express my emotions (anger, sadness, jealousy, etc.) in a healthy way through calm and respectful direct communication with that friend.

YES   NO   As long as my friend is eating healthy and getting some exercise, I believe that her body shape looks fine.

YES   NO   I know that I am a valuable person with positive qualities no matter who my friends are or even if I don't have any friends right now.

Tips For Being a Good Friend to Others and to Yourself

» Remember that your friend spending time with another friend does not mean that she does not want to be your friend. In the meantime, spend some time with other friends or spend some time with yourself doing activities that you like.

» To meet friends, join activities like school clubs where you will find people with interests similar to yours. Smile and/or make eye contact with people and have a few comments or questions to ask new people about.

» If you think you may want to spend less time with someone, start by gently explaining that you need some time for other activities. If this doesn't work, you may have to explain (gently) to the person that although you like her friendship, you need some space.

» Remember that good friends don't gossip about you but will tell a trusted adult or encourage you to get help if there is danger, will listen to you and allow you to listen to them, care about your well-being, don't change how they treat you based on other people's opinions, and sometimes agree to disagree.

» Is important to keep a balance between being a good friend to others and being true to yourself. Don't agree with someone when you really disagree, but don't force others to agree with you.

» Practice patience with people who are different from you. Experiment: Try not to argue with anyone or say anything rude for an entire day.

» Practice being direct by refraining from telling anyone else anything about another person (not gossiping) for an entire day.

» Practice appreciating rather than hating the differences in ourselves. This can help us to accept differences in others.

» List ten positive qualities that you have. These qualities can be big or small.

Dear Girl World...

This activity is best done with group members after they have completed most of the sessions. Write each scenario below on a separate notecard. Have group members pair up, give each pair a notecard, and have them read and brainstorm solutions for the writer for 5 minutes. Then have each pair read their notecard aloud to the group and tell the group what advice they would give the writer.

Notecard Problem Scenarios:

» My best friend doesn't want to sit next to me at lunch anymore. Help!

» I walk home with two friends every day. Lately, they are leaving without me so I have no one to walk home with! What do I do?

» All the girls I play with at recess act like they don't like me now. I don't know what happened or what to do!

» I just moved to a new school and I have no friends. I'm very lonely and I don't know how to fix this. Help!

» My best friend won't talk to me and is telling everyone she is mad at me. What do I do?

» I just heard an awful rumor that is going around school about me. How can I make it stop?

» A new girl just started at our school, and my best friend is spending more time with her than with me. I'm so upset! How can I get her back?

» I started a diet 3 months ago because I want to look more like the girls in teen magazines. But I haven't lost any weight yet. Help!

» I really want to start dating, but I'm not sure what the right age is to start. What do you think?

» A guy I have a crush on in math class talks to me about how dumb some of the other girls are in our class. I really want to talk to him and I know he wants me to make fun of them with him, but I feel guilty. It's not like the girls would ever find out, so is it really that bad?

» I just found out my friend's parents are getting a divorce, and she's angry all the time now. In fact, every time her parents have a bad fight at home, she fights in school the next day! How can I help her?

Cyberbully Role-play

Give each group member a chance to role-play her favorite strategy from Strategies to Avoid Cyberbullying (session three). The group leader can act as the person who is doing the cyberbullying so the group member has a chance to practice her strategy. It is best for the group leader to model a role-playing scenario first by choosing a volunteer and having her pretend to send a mean text message; then the group leader can act out strategy #4 to show how to handle the cyberbullying situation.

Handling Anger

This activity is very effective if you notice your group members struggling with unhealthy anger reactions or behaviors. Hand out the following "How Do You Handle Your Anger?" sheet and have group members read it aloud. After reading, ask group members which strategies they need explained further. Then have group members circle their favorite strategy on the sheet. Next, group members should write the strategy they circled on a notecard, framing it within the following goal prompt. The group leader should model this first. Have each group member read her notecard strategy aloud to the group. Finally, give each group member a chance to role-play her notecard strategy, with the group leader acting as the instigator (who/what) that makes that group member angry. For example, ask "Who wants to practice her strategy with me?" Then ask the volunteering group member, "What makes you angry at school?" If the group member says, "kids who kick my chair make me angry," then gently kick the group member's chair while coaching the group member to act out her notecard strategy. Be sure to spend a minute or two after each role-play briefly discussing how their strategy could be applied in a classroom setting. In closing, the group leader collects the notecards and photocopies them after group. Give the originals back to group members as a reminder to practice their strategies during the week, and keep the photocopies so that group members can share their successes with their strategies in the next group session.

How Do You Handle Your Anger?

Circle the anger strategy that will work best for YOU!

» Take time out and relax.

» Walk away from the problem.

» Write or draw your feelings on paper.

» Use humor and make a joke out of it.

» Convince yourself to LET IT GO!

» Talk it out with an "I" message.

» Say you are sorry and make up.

» Get help from an adult.

» Make a list of bad consequences of you getting angry.

Goal Prompt:

When I'm angry, I promise to try to: _____

_____ .

BOYS' VOICE
Boy Empowerment Group Counseling Guide

{ Table of Contents }

{ Boys' Voice Appendix }

Reproducible letters, forms, assessments and other materials contained in the digital files

» Parent Permission Letter

» Group Notes

» Group Evaluation

» Pre/Posttest

» Group Rules & Consequences

» Group Pass Examples

» Data Analysis

» Additional Activities

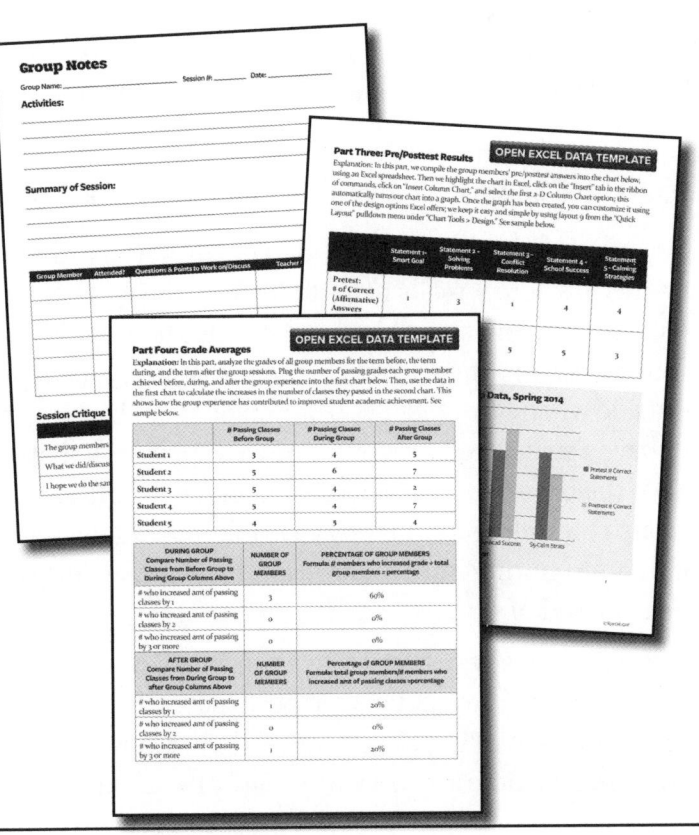

Recommendations Specific to Running a Boy Empowerment Counseling Group

Whenever I present to counselors and educators on facilitating psychoeducational groups, I always like to start with a "sparkling moment." A sparkling moment is that heartwarming time when you feel you have made a profound difference in the life of a child, or if you are very lucky, in the lives of many children. So, my sparkling moment came during a Boys' Voice group experience last year. I had invited our school resource officer (SRO) to co-lead the group with me in order to provide a male role model for the group members. I was nervous about having a police officer co-lead with me since most of the students in the group did not have positive experiences with law enforcement. They were our most disadvantaged boys who seemed to spend all of their time getting into trouble and going to the In-School Suspension room; also, many of them had incarcerated relatives. Well, I shouldn't have worried! Despite my reservations that these were THE most disrespectful kiddos in the school AND I was putting them in the same room with a police officer every week, the group went smashingly!

> Boy empowerment groups tend to be boisterous and high-energy, just like the boys themselves! So this is where it really helps to have a male co-leader who matches the boys' demographics, is charismatic, and also a bit younger in age to provide relatability.

Watching the relationship form between our SRO and the students was one of the highlights of my career. My boys, many of whom had no positive male role models in their lives, just hung on every word the SRO had to say and inhaled every grain of wisdom he shared, especially when he gently and tactfully answered all their questions about his uniform and gun that he wore to every group session. The bonding that I witnessed in these group sessions was sweet, inspiring and strong. I know this because the boys still come up to me from time to time to tell me how much they loved that group experience and how much they look forward to connecting with the SRO again when they see him at the high school, where he now works. And this makes me sparkle every time.

In addition to having a male co-leader that can serve as a role model for the group members, these are the suggested approaches that I have found work best with all Boys' Voice groups.

» Boy empowerment groups tend to be boisterous and high-energy, just like the boys themselves! So this is where it really helps to have a male co-leader who matches the boys' demographics, is charismatic, and also a bit younger in age to provide relatability. I've purposefully built lots of movement into the sessions because many boys can't sit still for long periods of time. So, take them outside whenever possible to do activities such as role-plays, Trashball, games, etc. It is important to have a structured, positive tone to the group activities with a lot of movement thrown in- this will keep the boys coming back session after session! Also, be aware that you may have to sell the idea of group counseling to your boys. I think counseling doesn't always have the biggest draw for boys, plus, if they are getting into trouble a lot, they likely won't want to focus on their troubles, which they may be ashamed of.

» It is sometimes necessary to do a continual, 8-week hard sell to get and, more importantly, to keep the boys in this group. This can be achieved by fostering the positive tone mentioned previously. Additionally, making the group "fun" can really help draw the boys in- you might "create the fun" by awarding on-time arrivals with healthy treats, giving prizes, being really enthusiastic during group sessions, giving group members any perks possible (such as "free" planners and school supplies), and praising them for the tiniest achievement towards their goal.

» Since boys can be a little rambunctious at times, four to six members is an ideal number of group participants.

» Sometimes group members are resistant to participating in role-play exercises. It is important to get everyone involved in role-playing so they can practice their skills in a safe environment. In order to get resistant group members involved in role-playing, try gently introducing the role-play strategy to the entire group by having the group first read and discuss the role-playing situations/scenarios together. Also, you might consider turning the role-play into a game by telling group members that they will vote on the best role-play at the end of the group session and that all the actors in the role-playing skit that receives the most votes will get a prize.

» I often have a follow-up session about a month or two after the group terminates to check in on group members' interpersonal experiences/successes. During the follow-up session, I generally follow these steps:

- Take attendance and review group rules (included in Appendix).
- Ask group members what issues or recent situations they want to discuss relating to boy issues.
- Review the Four Steps to Conflict Resolution and have each group member select a conflict card (included with session seven). Have them each read the card aloud and then role-play using the four conflict resolution steps while the group leader (or a partner, if members can handle this) "bothers" the member with the conflict card behavior.
- Review the Healthy Coping Skills (included with session two) and ask how each member is remembering to use their preferred coping skill in difficult times.
- Finally, play Goals Bingo from the Additional Activities with group members (included in Appendix).

American School Counselor Association Standards Alignment

The American School Counselor Association (ASCA) sets the national framework for a model school counseling program. As a result, the Boys' Voice session activities are aligned with the following ASCA Mindsets & Behaviors that can be applied to the domains of Academic Development and Personal/Social Development.

Mindsets

M 2.	Self-confidence in ability to succeed
M 3.	Sense of belonging in the school environment
M 5.	Belief in using abilities to their fullest to achieve high-quality results and outcomes
M 6.	Positive attitude toward work and learning

Behaviors

B-LS 1.	Demonstrate critical-thinking skills to make informed decisions
B-SMS 1.	Demonstrate ability to assume responsibility
B-SS 1.	Use effective oral and written communication skills and listening skills
B-LS 2.	Demonstrate creativity
B-SMS 2.	Demonstrate self-discipline and self-control
B-SS 2.	Create positive and supportive relationships with other students
B-SS 4.	Demonstrate empathy
B-SMS 5.	Demonstrate perseverance to achieve long- and short-term goals
B-SS 5.	Demonstrate ethical decision-making and social responsibility
B-SS 6.	Use effective collaboration and cooperation skills
B-SMS 7.	Demonstrate effective coping skills when faced with a problem
B-SS 7.	Use leadership and teamwork skills to work effectively in diverse teams
B-SS 8.	Demonstrate advocacy skills and ability to assert self, when necessary
B-SMS 9.	Demonstrate personal safety skills
B-SS 9.	Demonstrate social maturity and behaviors appropriate to the situation and environment
B-SMS 10.	Demonstrate ability to manage transitions and ability to adapt to changing situations and responsibilities

Boys' Voice
Session One: Making SMART Goals

Topic Overview

The group member will:

» Make introductions with other group members

» Identify the purpose of the group

» Discuss group rules/norms

» Identify some commonalities with other group members

» Identify the components of a SMART goal

» Make a SMART goal for success in school

Materials

» Reproducibles: *The Candy Introductions Game, SMART Goal Poster, Goal Stem & Prompts*

» Coloring Mandala, Chart Paper, Different Colored Candies, Note Cards, Markers or Crayons, Pencils

» Your selected items from the Appendix in the digital files

Procedures

Reminder – These session procedures will take about 1 hour to complete, so feel free to shorten or lengthen the session according to your time constraints. For ideas on how to do this, see the Recommendations for Starting a Counseling Group located at the beginning of this book. Of course, the more experienced you are with facilitating groups and with using this group curriculum, the more efficiently and quickly you will be able to guide group members through the procedures below.

1. Take attendance on the Group Notes sheet (included in Appendix) and offer students a coloring mandala from the Additional Activities section as a warmup activity to do as they are waiting for others to enter and the group session to start.

2. Ask group members what they think they will learn about in this group and guide them to the idea that the purpose of the group is to encourage each other as they achieve their goals to become strong leaders, build friendships, and be successful in school.

3. Show the rules poster (included in Appendix), and have each group member read a rule aloud and share what he thinks the rule means. Remember to always remind group members that they can say "pass" if they do not want to read aloud.

4. Show the directions to *The Candy Introductions Game*. After reviewing instructions, hand out a few colored candies to each group member and have group members introduce themselves by playing. Then have members play the game by stating their name, age, and information based on the colors of the candies they have. You should go first to model this for group members.

5. Hand out the pretest (included in Appendix) and read aloud as group members fill in Yes/No for each statement. Collect and save these pretests until the last group session.

6. Display the *SMART Goal Poster*. Tell group members that they will now create a SMART goal for themselves. Briefly explain what a SMART goal is by pointing out what each of the capital letters stands for on the *SMART Goal Poster*.

7. Have group members think about one thing that is not going well for them at school and how they would like to improve it- use the "think-aloud" strategy to model this first; a think-aloud is when you verbalize out loud what you are thinking during each step of your thought process so members can observe how you identify what is not going well at school and then how you will improve it.

8. Show members the Goal Stem template and have them copy it on a note card and fill in their SMART goal in the goal stem blank. Be sure to model this first. Also, display and point out the Goal Prompts that they can copy if they can't think of a goal on their own.

Supplemental Forms and Handouts for Session One
(In Appendix in the digital files)
» Parent Permission Letter
» Group Notes Sheet
» Group Evaluation
» Pre/Post Test
» Group Rules & Consequences
» Group Pass Examples
» Data Analysis
» Additional Activities

9. Next, have each group member read their goal aloud to the group while the group checks each goal to make sure it is SMART. To do this, after a member reads their goal, you should read each SMART goal component off the SMART Goal Poster while the group members give a thumbs up if the goal incorporates that component or a thumbs down if it does not incorporate the component.

10. If the group determines that a group member's goal does not incorporate one (or more) of the SMART components, ask the group how the group member should modify their goal so all components are included. Choose a proficient group member to help the struggling member change their goal, if necessary.

11. Collect the goal note cards. Photocopy the note cards after group and give group members a copy the following day as a reminder to work toward their SMART goal during the week. Keep the originals for the next group session.

12. Optional Homework Activity: Tell group members the following, "Talk with a family member about your goal. Notice their reaction to your goal because we will talk about this during the next session."

13. Complete the group evaluation (included in Appendix). To do this, the group leader reads each evaluation statement aloud, and group members hold up fingers to indicate whether they agree/disagree/feel "sort of" about each statement. The group leader tallies group members' responses in each Agree/Sort of/Disagree column on the Group Notes sheet (included in Appendix) for use in planning the next session.

Sometimes this initial session can run a bit long, taking the full hour. If necessary, you can stop the session after students write on their goal note card and then continue with activities eight through twelve above in the following session.

Discussion Questions

» What are you most excited about learning or doing in this group? Explain.

» What are you most nervous about learning or doing in this group? Explain.

» Why did you choose the SMART goal you wrote on your card?

The Candy Introductions Game

This is a fun icebreaker to help your group members loosen up and get to know each other a little better. Read over the directions below with group members and then model each direction for them. Finally, distribute a few different colored candies to each group member and have the group play the game in round-robin fashion. You can also have the candies placed in individual plastic bags ahead of time.

Directions:

» The group leader will hand out a few candies to each group member. You can eat your candies AFTER the game.

» Look at your candy colors and the chart below to learn what you should tell the group about yourself.

» When it is your turn, say your name and age and tell the group information about yourself based on your candy colors.

If you have a GREEN CANDY:
Tell the group the best part of your day.

If you have a BROWN CANDY:
Tell the group the worst part of your day.

If you have a RED CANDY:
Tell the group something that really stresses you out.

If you have a BLUE CANDY:
Tell the group something that calms you down.

If you have an ORANGE CANDY:
Tell the group about a good decision you made this week.

If you have a YELLOW CANDY:
Tell the group about a poor decision you made this week.

If you have a PINK CANDY:
Tell the group about something that makes you mad.

If you have a PURPLE CANDY:
Tell the group something interesting about you.

If you have a WHITE CANDY:
Tell the group about a goal you have for yourself this year.

If you have a BLACK CANDY:
Tell the group about something you like to do for fun.

SMART Goal Poster

(S)= Specific

Exactly what do you want to achieve?

(M)= Measureable

What is the proof that you will see when you achieve your goal?

(A)= Achievable

Can you realistically achieve your goal?

(R)= Relevant

Is your goal worthwhile for you to achieve?

(T)= Time Bound

When will you achieve your goal?

Goal Stem and Prompts

Goal Stem Template

My goal for being successful in school this week is to:

_____ .

Goal Prompts

Pass my math class

Finish completing my college application

Raise my hand before speaking in class

Follow my teacher's directions

Keep my hands to myself

Complete my homework every night

Look at/listen to the teacher in class

Have my school supplies with me at school

Ask for help when I don't understand

Use respectful language with my peers

Use respectful language with my teachers

Arrive to class on-time

Keep my school work neatly organized in my binder

Goal Success Sharing Steps (to be used next session):

1. Read your goal aloud.

2. Give an example of your success with the goal.

Boys' Voice
Session Two: How Healthy are Your Coping Skills?

Topic Overview

The group member will:

» Discuss his success with his goal

» Identify and compare healthy and unhealthy coping skills

» Choose his favorite healthy coping skill

» Apply a muscle-relaxation technique as a healthy coping skill to manage stress

Materials

» Reproducibles: *Goal Success Sharing Steps Poster, Healthy Coping Skills, Muscle Makeover, Coping Skills Bingo*

» Note Cards, Coloring Mandala, Pencils, Bingo Chips or Pebbles, Pencils, Markers or Crayons

» Your selected items from the Appendix in the digital files

Procedures

1. Take attendance on the Group Notes sheet (included in Appendix) and offer students a coloring mandala from the Additional Activities section to keep them occupied as other members arrive.

2. Show the rules poster (included in Appendix), and have each group member read a rule aloud. Remember to always remind group members that they can say "pass" if they do not want to read aloud.

3. Homework Shareout: Ask group members to share their family members' reactions to their goals.

4. If you didn't finish the goal work in session one, take time now to complete activities nine and ten from session one. Then skip to activity eight below.

5. Alternately, if you did finish the goal work in the last session, hand out the photocopies of the goal note cards. Show group members the *Goal Success Sharing Steps* poster and model how to do steps 1 and 2. For example, you can read off, "My goal for being successful in school this week is to pass my math class," from your goal note card that you modeled making in the last session. Then you can tell the group, "When I checked my grades with my teacher yesterday, I had a 66% in math, but I passed my math test yesterday so that is a success."

6. Give group members 1 minute to think of a success they had in the past week with the goal on their note card.

7. Allow each group member to present their *Goal Success Sharing Steps* to the group.

8. Discuss with group members the definition of coping skills and briefly discuss the difference between healthy versus unhealthy coping skills.

9. Distribute the *Healthy Coping Skills* list and have group members read it in a round-robin fashion.

After the group has finished reading, ask group members on which skills they need further explanation. Have each group member circle his favorite one and then copy it onto the bottom of his goal note card so he remembers what it is in order to do his session homework. Collect the goal note cards. Photocopy the note cards after group and give group members a copy the following day as a reminder to work toward their SMART goal and practice their coping skill during the week. Keep the originals for the next group session.

10. If time, do one of the following activities below:

> » Tell members that now you are going to teach them a healthy coping skill that falls under the "exercise" category. Distribute the *Muscle Makeover* directions sheet and give everyone a chance to review it. Have everyone stand and shake out their arms and legs and walk around a bit to get the blood flowing. Choose one group member to read the *Muscle Makeover* directions aloud while you model following each of the directions for the group. Finally, have members practice the relaxation strategy with you.

> » Hand out a *Coping Skills Bingo* template to each group member. Have group members copy the bolded healthy coping skills words from their handout onto the Bingo template in any random order. Play *Coping Skills Bingo*. It is a good idea to play this in future sessions during the last 5–10 minutes of group so that group members keep the coping skills fresh in their minds.

> **Supplemental Forms and Handouts for Session Two**
> (In Appendix in the digital files)
> » Group Notes Sheet
> » Group Evaluation
> » Group Rules & Consequences
> » Group Pass Examples
> » Data Analysis
> » Additional Activities

11. Optional Homework Activity: Ask group members to use their circled coping skill that they wrote at the bottom of their goal note card between now and the next session whenever they experience negative feelings. Tell them that they will share their experiences with using the coping skills during the next session.

12. Complete the group evaluation (included in Appendix). To do this, the group leader reads each evaluation statement aloud, and group members hold up fingers to indicate whether they agree/disagree/feel "sort of" about each statement. The group leader tallies group members' responses in each Agree/Sort of/Disagree column on the Group Notes sheet (included in Appendix) for use in planning the next session.

Discussion Questions

» What are you most proud of with your goal success? Why?

» Do you know someone who uses unhealthy coping skills? What do you think of this?

» How did you feel during *Muscle Makeover*? Explain how you found it helpful or unhelpful.

Goal Success Sharing Steps Poster

Read your goal aloud.

1

Give an example of your success with the goal.

2

Healthy Coping Skills

Definition

Coping skills are the ways that we handle difficult moments in our lives such as a bad memory, getting in trouble, failing a test, a relationship breakup, etc.

A Few Examples of Healthy Versus Unhealthy Coping Skills

Healthy	Unhealthy
Vent to a friend	Yell at someone
Take a walk	Fight
Play a Sport	Take drugs

Top Ten Healthy Coping Skills

Vent to a friend/family member.

Exercise.

Make a **plan** for how to solve/handle what's bothering you.

Look for the **positive** in your situation.

Be creative: **Draw! Paint! Sing! Act!**

Substitute a good behavior for the one that is bothering you.

Meditate or do relaxation exercises.

Spend time with your **pet**(s).

Talk to a **counselor** or another adult.

Eat well and **sleep** well.

Discussion Questions (if time)

Which healthy coping skills above are unclear to you?

Circle your favorite coping skill. Why is it your favorite?

What is an example of an unhealthy coping skill? What makes it unhealthy?

Role-play one of the coping skills above with a partner. Be sure to spend a minute or two after each role-play briefly discussing how their strategy could be applied in a classroom setting.

Muscle Makeover

This strategy involves a clenching and releasing of five muscle groups. It's a muscle relaxation exercise that members can do anywhere—even sitting in a chair during a test in a classroom!

{ Here are the steps for the group members to follow: }

1 | Sit upright in your chair.

2 | Scrunch up your entire face like you just smelled something really bad: eyes squeezed shut, mouth puckered, nose crinkled, etc. Hold for 5 seconds and then let your entire face relax into a calm expression. Repeat four times.

3 | Clench your fists as tight as you can and hold for 5 seconds, then release. Repeat four times.

4 | Push your arms out at about a 35 degree angle from your body, stretching them and reaching down as far as you can. Hold for 5 seconds and then release to let your arms fall gently at your sides. Repeat four times.

5 | Push the soles of your feet into the floor as hard as you can, holding onto your chair or desk for leverage. Hold for 5 seconds and release, relaxing your legs. Repeat four times.

6 | Curl your toes inside your shoes as tight as you can, holding for 5 seconds. Then release your toes to lie flat in your shoes. Repeat four times.

Coping Skills Bingo

Hand out the bingo template below to each group member. Have group members copy the bolded words of the healthy coping skills listed in the Healthy Coping Skills list onto the bingo template in any random order. Play *Coping Skills Bingo* by following the directions below. It is a good idea to play this during the last 5–10 minutes of every group session if your members are having trouble remembering healthy coping skills, as mine often do. *If your group members are very young, you might give them pre-printed bingo cards with the coping skills already filled in.*

1. Call out a bingo letter and coping skill.

2. Repeat the bingo letter and skill.

3. If a group member has that combination of bingo letter and skill, he can put a marker (bean or pebble) in the correct spot on the bingo card.

4. The first group member to get five beans/pebbles placed in a row or column calls out "BINGO" and wins a prize. After someone wins, have group members clear their cards of game pieces and start again.

5. Collect the bingo cards after the game to be handed out again for a future game.

B	I	N	G	O
		FREE SPACE ☺		

Boys' Voice

Session Three: The Problem with the Masculine Stereotype

Topic Overview

The group member will:

» Practice mindfulness with the *Mindful Minute* Activity

» Discuss his success with his goal

» Identify and analyze masculine stereotypes

» Play *Stereotype Trash Ball* to dispel unfair or untrue stereotypes

» Review his coping skills knowledge with the *Coping Skills Bingo* game

Materials

» Reproducibles: *Mindful Minute, Masculine Stereotype Vignette, Masculine Stereotype Discussion Questions, Stereotype Trashball Cards, Goal Success Sharing Steps* poster (from last session), *Healthy Coping Skills* (from last session), *Coping Skills Bingo* (from last session)

» Note Cards, Trashcan, Bell (or tone on phone), Pencils, Bingo Chips or Pebbles, and a Computer or DVD player (if you are showing a video clip in activity eight)

» Your selected items from the Appendix in the digital files

Procedures

1. Take attendance on the Group Notes sheet (included in Appendix). Ask group members whether there is anything they want to discuss relating to boy issues; guide them to limit responses/ discussions to 5–10 minutes (see the recommendations section for tips on keeping within these time constraints).

2. Show the rules poster (included in Appendix), and have each group member read a rule aloud. Remember to always remind group members that they can say "pass" if they do not want to read aloud.

3. Introduce boys to the *Mindful Minute* and lead them through the activity. This is a wonderful relaxation strategy that really starts the group off on a calm and collected note- it is good to include it in every session.

4. *Homework Shareout:* Review the *Healthy Coping Skills* (from last session) with group members and have each member tell again their favorite coping skill (that they wrote on their note card). Ask members to share a time during the past week when they used their coping skill to deal with a negative feeling.

5. *Goal Shareout:* Show group members the *Goal Success Sharing Steps* poster (from last session) and, if necessary, model how to do steps 1 and 2. For an example of this modeling, see session two. Give group members 1 minute to think of a success they had in the past week with their note card goal. Allow each group member to present the *Goal Success Sharing Steps* to the group. Ask group members if they feel their goal is still possible to achieve (reasonable) and important to them (relevant) or if they need to write a new goal. If necessary, give them time to write a new SMART goal.

Collect the goal note cards. Photocopy the note cards after group and give group members a copy the following day as a reminder to work toward their SMART goal during the week. Keep the originals for the next group session.

6. Show the *Stereotype Discussion Questions* and ask students what they think a stereotype is. Guide group members to understand the definition of a stereotype; also, give members an example of how stereotypes can be both positive and negative. Refer to the answer key of the *Stereotype Discussion Questions* for this information, if necessary.

7. Tell students to think about questions two and three of the *Stereotype Discussion Questions* while they watch a video clip or listen to a reading about masculine stereotypes.

8. Show students the video clip or read them the *Masculine Stereotype Vignette.*

9. Discuss each of the *Masculine Stereotype Discussion Questions* with the group. If the group members are very young, or if you are short on time, you might skip questions three through six and proceed instead to the more concrete and tactile *Stereotype Trash Ball* next.

> **Supplemental Forms and Handouts for Session Three**
> (In Appendix in the digital files)
> » Group Notes Sheet
> » Group Evaluation
> » Group Rules & Consequences
> » Group Pass Examples
> » Data Analysis
> » Additional Activities

10. Arrange the boys in a circle and give each boy a *Stereotype Trashball Card.* Have each student read their stereotype card aloud and then tell the group why it is unfair or untrue. Next, the student should crumple up the card and try to make a basketball shot into the trashcan in the middle of the circle; this is a symbol to the students that unfair or untrue stereotypes are just "trash." Make sure you go first in order to model the steps for the group.

11. If time, play *Coping Skills Bingo* (from last session). It is a good idea to play this in future sessions during the last 5–10 minutes of group so that group members keep the coping skills fresh in their minds.

12. Optional Homework Activity: Tell group members, "discuss masculine stereotypes with a member of your family. Notice your family member's reaction to this topic because we will talk about this during the next session."

13. Complete the group evaluation (included in Appendix). To do this, the group leader reads each evaluation statement aloud, and group members hold up fingers to indicate whether they agree/disagree/feel "sort of" about each statement. The group leader tallies group members' responses in each Agree/Sort of/Disagree column on the Group Notes sheet (included in Appendix) for use in planning the next session.

Discussion Questions

» How did it feel to crumple up the stereotype card and throw it in the trashcan during Stereotype Trashball? Explain.

» What is the stereotype of masculinity or what does it mean to be a "real man?"

» What kinds of things would boys have to do if they want to fit into the masculine stereotype (prove they are a "real man")?

Mindful Minute

Practicing mindfulness means becoming aware of your present moment, being conscious and aware of your experience in the present moment, without judging. In other words, just be, just breathe. One of the best ways to start this practice with group members is by explaining to them that you will ring a bell or play a tone and once they hear it, they should focus all their attention for one minute on their breathing. Their mind will wander off and when it does, they can gently return their attention to their breathing, again and again. Group members can put their heads down or leave them up – their choice. At the end of the minute, ring the bell or play the tone a second time to signal the end of the mindfulness exercise.

*Optional – Ask students to describe their experience with the Mindful Minute activity.

Masculine Stereotype Vignette

For the Counselor: During session three, you can choose whether to show students a video clip about masculinity or read the Masculine Stereotype Vignette below. If you choose to show a video clip, there are many websites where you can find video clips about the masculine stereotype. Type "masculine stereotype video" into an Internet search engine and select the "videos" tab. Then you can pick a video clip appropriate for the age group of your students from any of the choices there. Some of my favorite masculine stereotype video clips are *Tough Guise* by Jackson Katz, *I am Not a Label* by Prince Ea, *Boys Don't Cry* by the American Psychological Association, and *The Present* by Jacob Frey.

What is the Masculine Stereotype?

For the Student: A stereotype is an (often untrue) belief that many people have about all people/objects with a similar characteristic. Stereotypes can be both good and bad, but harmful stereotypes occur when we have ideas about people where we judge them without even knowing them. For example, if we judge people based on what they look like instead of taking the time to find out who they really are inside, we are making a big mistake!

The masculine stereotype is a widely accepted and oversimplified belief about the feelings and actions of boys and men, just because they are male. Here are some examples of the masculine stereotype:

» men are tough

» boys don't cry or show emotion

» the man is the head or boss of the family

» "real men" are physically strong or tall

» the man should make more money than the woman

» a boy who won't fight is weak

These examples above can definitely encourage negative stereotyping!

The masculine stereotype can lead people to judge a guy just because he is male, before they even get to know him! These stereotypes about what men are supposed to be like are in lots of places. Here is a list of where we might find the masculine stereotype:

Religion • Culture • Books • Magazines • TV Shows • TV Commercials • Movies • Parents and Teachers • Our Friends • School Rules • Music Lyrics

Where else can you find the masculine stereotype?

High School Students Jeff, Tyrone, and Aurelio Talk about the Masculine Stereotype

Jeff – Stereotypes aren't very accurate. Is it really true that all men should be taller than women? Or that only men have muscles? Or that men shouldn't do the cooking at home? Do gender stereotypes even matter? No! Stereotypes about males and females aren't always true! They're just assumptions about what we should to be like, but not who we really are. For example, my brother is short so I think boys can be short. Or my mom works late, so my dad makes dinner. And some girls are stronger than me!

Tyrone – We can challenge masculine stereotypes and it's important to do so because many times they are not true! These stereotypes can make a boy feel like someone is putting a wall around who he can be and what he can do! It is like someone is trying to put you in a category or a box and no one wants to be put in a box! Real people are also a lot more complex and interesting than stereotypes.

Aurelio – The whole "men are supposed to be strong, aggressive, and unemotional" is really hard. Both girls and boys can be emotional – I'm a boy and I'm sensitive and caring about other people. Just because I am a boy doesn't mean that I shouldn't be those things. The masculine stereotype is bad because it can make boys feel like they have to hide their feelings and pretend to be something they are not, or be tough in how they treat other people. This is unhealthy and can lead to mental problems.

Tyrone – Putting people into categories sends a message that there are ways girls and boys "should" behave. That can be really hard if we are feeling boxed in by other people's expectations and judgements about how males and females are supposed to act. People are much more interesting than a stereotype. In reality, people can be so many different things!

Jeff – Yea, I try to use the masculine stereotype for good in my life. Like, it makes me think twice about if people are stereotyping me, and this helps me to choose to do things based on what I think is important and not on what they expect me to do. I love to figure skate on ice and I'm usually the only boy in the ice skating lesson, but I don't mind. And occasionally when I do feel weird about this, I just remind myself that I am bursting through the masculine stereotype with my triple lutz jumps!

Masculine Stereotype Discussion Questions with Answer Key

1. **What is a stereotype?**

» A belief (maybe untrue) that many people have about all people/objects with a similar characteristic.

» A belief that helps people to decide how to judge an object/experience in life; stereotypes can be helpful when people need to separate dogs from cats or a snake from a twig. Stereotyping is not always "wrong," and, in some cases, it is a natural part of life.

2. **What exactly is the masculine stereotype or what does it mean to be a "real man?"**

» Thinking that all men have (or must have) the following characteristics- tough, violent, brave, physically strong, not showing feelings, not crying, aggressive.

3. **How can the masculine stereotype of acting like a "real man" be harmful or unhealthy for guys?**

» It can lead boys to feel ashamed if they don't have certain characteristics.

» It can cause boys to keep feelings bottled in which is mentally unhealthy for any human.

» It can create pressure to do unhealthy things like fight and drink.

4. **What can you do to challenge or overcome these stereotypes?**

» Be proud of YOUR characteristics whatever they are.

» Teach others to avoid stereotyping.

» Accept people as they are.

5. **Give examples of positive and negative stereotypes.**

» Positive – Women are caring so if you are in danger, go to a woman. Don't touch that snake – it's dangerous!

» Negative – All men are (have to be) strong. Women aren't tough (so they can't be in the military).

6. **What kinds of things would guys have to do if they want to fit into the masculine stereotype (prove they are a "real man")?**

» Fight, act tough, not show feelings, not cry, have big muscles, etc.

Stereotype Trashball Cards

Directions: Cut up these cards and put them in a jar to use in the session three Stereotype Trashball Game.

Boys should never cry.	It's ok for boys to fight because that's the way men settle their problems.
All boys are tough and like sports.	The man should always pay for dinner.
It is bad for boys to play with dolls.	A short man is weak.
Men shouldn't cook—that is a job for a woman.	Men who are strong and tall are real men.
Only men should be soldiers because men like war.	Boys who don't like sports are sissies.

Boys' Voice
Session Four: Solutions for the Masculine Stereotype

Topic Overview

The group member will:

» Practice mindfulness with the Mindful Minute Activity

» Discuss his success with his goal

» Identify and analyze masculine stereotypes through the Masculine Box activity

» Challenge masculine stereotypes and celebrate his individuality with a Masculine Shield

Materials

» Reproducibles: *Mindful Minute* (from last session), *Masculine Stereotype Discussion Questions* (from last session), *Goal Success Sharing Steps* poster (from session two)

» Note Cards, a Bell (or tone on phone), Construction or Butcher Paper, Markers or Crayons, Thumbtacks, Scissors, Glue, Pencils, and Magazines

» Your selected items from the Appendix in the digital files

Procedures

1. Take attendance on the Group Notes sheet (included in Appendix). Ask group members whether there is anything they want to discuss relating to boy issues; guide them to limit responses/discussions to 5–10 minutes (see the recommendations section for tips on keeping within these time constraints).

2. Show the rules poster (included in Appendix), and have each group member read a rule aloud. Remember to always remind group members that they can say "pass" if they do not want to read aloud.

3. Do the *Mindful Minute* Activity (from last session).

4. *Homework Shareout:* Ask members to share their family reactions to the masculine stereotype.

5. *Goal Shareout:* Show group members the *Goal Success Sharing Steps* and, if necessary, model how to do steps 1 and 2. For an example of this modeling, see session two. Give group members one minute to think of a success they had in the past week with their note card goal. Allow each group member to present the steps to the group. If anyone wants to change or add a second SMART goal (and they have achieved their first goal), allow some time for this. Collect the goal note cards. Photocopy the note cards after group and give group members a copy the following day as a reminder to work toward their SMART goal during the week. Keep the originals for the next group session.

6. Quickly review the answers to a few of the *Stereotype Discussion Questions* (from last session) with the group.

7. Spread out a large sheet of construction or butcher paper on the group table so all group members can access it. With a marker, write the words "Masculine Box" in the middle of the paper with a box drawn around it. Write some words inside the box that fit the masculine stereotype (tough, strong,

no emotions, etc.). Ask students to write additional words inside the box that come to mind when they think of the masculine stereotype or what a "real man" is.

8. Now ask students to write words outside of the box that boys are called if they do not fit the masculine stereotype; it is best to model some examples to get them started like "wimp," "weakling," "mama's boy," etc.)

9. Hang the *Masculine Box* on the wall. Ask students to share their opinions of it.

10. If time, members can make and share a *Masculinity Shield* from the Additional Activities section (included in Appendix).

11. *Optional Homework Activity:* Tell group members, "Pay careful attention to television and/or movies this week and look for evidence of masculine stereotypes in the media. We will discuss your observations about this during the next session."

12. Complete the group evaluation (included in Appendix). To do this, the group leader reads each evaluation statement aloud, and group members hold up fingers to indicate whether they agree/disagree/feel "sort of" about each statement. The group leader tallies group members' responses in each Agree/Sort of/Disagree column on the Group Notes sheet (included in Appendix) for use in planning the next session.

> **Supplemental Forms and Handouts for Session Four**
> (In Appendix in the digital files)
>
> » Group Notes Sheet
> » Group Evaluation
> » Group Rules & Consequences
> » Group Pass Examples
> » Data Analysis
> » Additional Activities

Discussion Questions

» Overall, how is your SMART goal working out for you? What could you do to improve yourself even more?

» Describe the best part of making your *Masculine Shield*.

» Do you feel like you are getting better on focusing only on your breaths during *Mindful Minute*? Why or why not?

Boys' Voice
Session Five: Handling Anger

Topic Overview

The group member will:

» Practice mindfulness with the Mindful Minute Activity

» Discuss his success with his goal

» Learn about various anger management strategies and choose the one that works best for him

» Apply various anger management strategies in a game called "Cool It!"

Materials

» Reproducibles: *Anger Management Strategies, Cool It game, Goal Success Sharing Steps* poster (from session two)

» Note Cards, Bell (or tone on phone), Pencils, Dice, Small Box or Jar, and a Small Prize

» Your selected items from the Appendix in the digital files

Procedures

1. Take attendance on the Group Notes sheet (included in Appendix). Ask group members whether there is anything they want to discuss relating to boy issues; guide them to limit responses/discussions to 5–10 minutes.

2. Show the rules poster (included in Appendix), and have each group member read a rule aloud. Remember to always remind group members that they can say "pass" if they do not want to read aloud.

3. Do the *Mindful Minute* Activity (from session three).

4. *Homework Shareout:* Ask group members to share what kinds of masculine stereotypes they noticed on television or in the movies and how they feel about this.

5. *Goal Shareout:* Show group members the *Goal Success Sharing Steps* (from session two) and, if necessary, model how to do steps 1 and 2. For an example of this modeling, see session two. Give group members 1 minute to think of a success they had in the past week with their note card goal. Allow each group member to present the steps to the group. If anyone wants to change or add a second SMART goal (and they have achieved their first goal), allow some time for this.

6. Hand out an *Anger Management Strategies* sheet to each group member and read it in a round-robin fashion. After the group has finished reading, ask group members on which numbers they need further explanation. Have group members circle and share with the group the anger management strategy that they think will work best for them.

7. Have the group members copy their preferred anger management strategy onto their goal note card so they remember what it is in order to do their session homework. Collect the goal note cards. Photocopy the note cards after group and give group members a copy the following day as a reminder

to work toward their SMART goal during the week. Keep the originals for the next group session. Also collect the *Anger Management Strategies* sheets for use in the next session.

8. Introduce and play *Cool It!* with group members.

9. *Optional Homework Activity:* Instruct group members to do the following, "As you're spending time with people over the next week, practice your chosen anger management strategy when you feel mad. Pay attention to how/whether your strategy calms you down and keeps you out of trouble. We'll talk about this during the next session."

10. Complete the group evaluation (included in Appendix). To do this, the group leader reads each evaluation statement aloud, and group members hold up fingers to indicate whether they agree/disagree/feel "sort of" about each statement. The group leader tallies group members' responses in each Agree/Sort of/Disagree column on the Group Notes sheet (included in Appendix) for use in planning the next session.

Discussion Questions

» Do you think anger is harming your body? If so, how?

» What object best represents your anger? Explain.

» Did you like the "Cool It!" game? Why or why not?

Supplemental Forms and Handouts for Session Five
(In Appendix in the digital files)

» Group Notes Sheet

» Group Evaluation

» Group Rules & Consequences

» Group Pass Examples

» Data Analysis

» Additional Activities

Anger Management Strategies

Circle the anger management strategy that will work best for YOU!

1. Take time out and relax.
Count to ten. Take five deep breaths. Feel yourself go all rubbery.

2. Walk away from the problem.
Go to a safe place.

3. Write or draw your feelings on paper.
Make pictures or words showing how you feel.

4. Use humor. Make a joke out of it.
Think of something funny about what happened or laugh at yourself.

5. Think: it's no big deal. Convince yourself to LET IT GO!
Decide if the problem is worth getting upset over.

6. Talk it out. Use "I" messages.
Tell the person/group how you feel OR tell them to stop in a serious way.

7. Say you are sorry and make up.
Only do this if you really mean it.

8. Get help from an adult.
Or ask another student to mediate.

9. Make a list of bad consequences of you getting angry.
Read the list to calm yourself and control your anger.

10. Your own anger management strategy:

_____

The Cool It! Game

Materials:
Anger Management Strategies (cut out the strategies on the next page so that each strategy is on an individual slip of paper), decorated box, set of dice, chips (optional)

Directions:

(1) Fold the slips of paper showing the anger management strategies and put them in the box.

(2) With group members standing in a circle, have a group member take one strategy from the box and roll the dice.

    a. If they roll an even number, they must give an example of a time that they used the strategy and how they felt as they used it. If the group member has never used the strategy, they can describe a situation where they might use it in the future.

    b. If they roll an odd number, the group member on their right must give an example.

    c. If they roll doubles, the entire group must discuss the strategy and share their experiences with using it.

(3) After the first group member has taken their turn, have the next group member take a turn, moving in a clockwise position.

(4) Continue playing until everyone has had two or three turns.

(5) If group members can handle it, give them a chip each time they are able to give an example of a time they used the strategy or would use the strategy in the future. This really motivates them to rack their brains and talk about their successes with anger management strategies. The group member with the most chips at the end of the game can win a small prize.

Anger Management
Strategies

Take time out and relax.	Make a joke out of it.
Count to ten.	Laugh at yourself.
Take five deep breaths.	Tell them to stop in a serious way.
Feel yourself go all rubbery.	Make up with the person.
Walk away from the problem.	Distract yourself by talking to a friend.
Go to a safe place.	Write your feelings on paper.
Ask another student to mediate.	Use humor.
Get help from an adult.	Say you're sorry.
Think about how it's no big deal.	Tell how you feel.
Convince yourself to LET IT GO!	Use "I" messages.
Make angry pictures showing how you feel.	Think of something funny about what happened.
Make a list of bad consequences of you getting angry.	Read your consequences list to calm yourself and control your anger.

Boys' Voice
Session Six: Acting Out Your Anger

Topic Overview

The group member will:

» Practice mindfulness with the *Mindful Minute* Activity

» Discuss his success with his goal

» Role-play his chosen anger management strategy

» Apply various anger management strategies or coping skills in a game

Materials

» Reproducibles: *Anger Management Strategies* (from last session), *Cool It Game* or *Coping Skills Bingo* (from previous sessions), *Goal Success Sharing Steps* poster (from session two)

» Chart Paper, Note Cards, a Bell (or Tone on Phone), Pencils, Bingo Chips or Pebbles, Dice, Small Box or Jar, a Small Prize

» Your selected items from the Appendix in the digital files

Procedures

1. Take attendance on the Group Notes sheet (included in Appendix). Ask group members whether there is anything they want to discuss relating to boy issues; guide them to limit responses/discussions to 5–10 minutes.

2. Show the rules poster (included in Appendix), and have each group member read a rule aloud. Remember to always remind group members that they can say "pass" if they do not want to read aloud.

3. Do the *Mindful Minute* Activity (from session three).

4. *Homework Shareout:* Ask group members to share how/whether their preferred anger management strategy (that they wrote on their goal note card) calmed them down and kept them out of trouble.

5. *Goal Shareout:* Show group members the *Goal Success Sharing Steps* (from session two) and, if necessary, model how to do steps 1 and 2. For an example of this modeling, see session two. Give group members 1 minute to think of a success they had in the past week with their note card goal. Allow each group member to present the steps to the group. If anyone wants to change or add a second SMART goal (and they have achieved their first goal), allow some time for this.

   At this point, if your group members don't need a second day of anger management activities, skip numbers six through eight. Instead, you can do the Dear Boys' Voice Experts activity from the Additional Activities section (see Appendix).

6. Hand out the *Anger Management Strategies* sheets from the last session. Have group members read the strategies aloud in a round-robin fashion to review. Ask students if anyone wants to change their preferred anger management strategy that they circled in the last session.

7. Have each group member role-play the anger management strategy on their note card, with you acting as the instigator (who/what) who makes that group member angry. For example, ask "Who wants to practice their strategy with me?" Then ask the volunteering group member, "What makes you angry at school?" If the group member says, "Kids who kick my chair make me angry," then gently kick the group member's chair while coaching them to act out the anger management strategy on their note card. Be sure to spend a minute or two after each role-play briefly discussing how their strategy could be applied in a classroom setting.

8. Collect the goal note cards. Allow students to take the *Anger Management Strategies* sheets home. Photocopy the note cards after group and give group members a copy the following day as a reminder to work toward their SMART goal and practice their anger management strategy during the week. Keep the originals for the next group session.

9. If time, play *Cool It!* or *Coping Skills Bingo* (from the previous sessions) with group members.

Supplemental Forms and Handouts for Session Six
(In Appendix in the digital files)

» Group Notes Sheet

» Group Evaluation

» Group Rules & Consequences

» Group Pass Examples

» Data Analysis

» Additional Activities

10. Optional Homework Activity: Instruct group members to do the following, "Talk to your family about the anger management strategy you're using. Show them your *Anger Management Strategy* Sheet. Tell them how it's working for you, and ask them what strategy calms them down. We'll talk about this during the next session."

11. Complete the group evaluation (included in Appendix). To do this, the group leader reads each evaluation statement aloud, and group members hold up fingers to indicate whether they agree/disagree/feel "sort of" about each statement. The group leader tallies group members' responses in each Agree/Sort of/Disagree column on the Group Notes sheet (included in Appendix) for use in planning the next session.

Discussion Questions

» What would you advise your family member to do if they were struggling with anger problems?

» How did you feel while role-playing your anger management strategy? Explain.

» Do you think boys or girls have more of a problem with anger management? Explain your answer.

Boys' Voice
Session Seven: The Four Steps of Conflict Resolution

Topic Overview

The group member will:

» Practice mindfulness with the *Mindful Minute* Activity

» Discuss his success with his goal

» Analyze a conflict resolution scenario

» Use "I" messages to communicate feelings and needs in a nonthreatening way

» Use the four steps of conflict resolution to solve an interpersonal problem

Materials

» Reproducibles: *Conflict Resolution, Goal Success Sharing Steps* Poster (from session two)

» Chart Paper, Markers, Note Cards, a Bell (or Tone on Phone), Pencils, a Jar

» Your selected items from the Appendix in the digital files

Procedures

1. Take attendance on the Group Notes sheet (included in Appendix). Ask group members whether there is anything they want to discuss relating to boy issues; guide them to limit responses/discussions to 5–10 minutes. Discuss with the group that the next session will be the last scheduled session. Tell group members that they can meet with you individually on an as-needed basis and give them the procedures for requesting this. In addition, ask them whether they would like a follow-up group session in one month and, if so, schedule it. See the recommendations section at the beginning of this guide for tips and content suggestions for the follow-up session.

2. Show the rules poster (included in Appendix), and have each group member read a rule aloud. Remember to always remind group members that they can say "pass" if they do not want to read aloud.

3. Do the *Mindful Minute* Activity (from session three).

4. *Homework Shareout:* Ask group members to share their family members' reactions to their preferred anger management strategy and what strategy their family member uses.

5. *Goal Shareout:* Show group members the *Goal Success Sharing Steps* (from session two) and, if necessary, model how to do steps 1 and 2. For an example of this modeling, see session two. Give group members 1 minute to think of a success they had in the past week with their note card goal. Allow each group member to present the steps to the group. If anyone wants to change or add a second SMART goal (and they have achieved their first goal), allow some time for this.

6. Introduce healthful ways to handle conflict by reading the *Conflict Scenario* to group members and then lead a brief discussion to answer the questions after the scenario.

7. Show the *Four Steps to Conflict Resolution* on chart paper and discuss each step. Ask group members how they have already used these steps in their lives. The group leader should model each of the steps

for the group while a volunteer kicks the group leader's chair as the "bothering" action. Discuss how steps one through three should only be used in minor conflicts; tell group members that anytime someone threatens them or puts their hands on them, they should go straight to step four.

8. Role-play each conflict resolution step with group members. Have a group member pick a Conflict Card from the jar and read the card to the group leader, who will then act out the card behavior in order to "bother" that group member. In this way, the group member can practice using each of the four steps to deal with the bothering person. Repeat with each group member.

   If your group members need more practice using the four steps of conflict resolution, you can add an additional session and use the expanded part of the Dear Boys' Voice Experts in Additional Activities (included in Appendix) to give members more conflict resolution practice.

9. Optional Homework Activity: Ask group members to practice using the four conflict resolution steps between now and the next session whenever they have an interpersonal conflict. Briefly brainstorm some conflicts that are interpersonal (for example, an argument with a friend) and some conflicts that are not interpersonal (for example, falling off your bike). Tell group members that they will share their experiences with the four conflict resolution steps at the beginning of the next session.

> ## Supplemental Forms and Handouts for Session Seven
> (In Appendix in the digital files)
>
> » Group Notes Sheet
> » Group Evaluation
> » Group Rules & Consequences
> » Group Pass Examples
> » Data Analysis
> » Additional Activities

10. Complete the group evaluation (included in Appendix). To do this, the group leader reads each evaluation statement aloud, and group members hold up fingers to indicate whether they agree/disagree/feel "sort of" about each statement. The group leader tallies group members' responses in each Agree/Sort of/Disagree column on the Group Notes sheet (included in Appendix) for use in planning the next session."

   * Sometimes this session can run a bit long, taking the full hour, especially if group members are not able to quickly move through the Homework and Goal Shareouts. If necessary, you can finish the role-plays in the final session instead of playing Coping Skills Bingo.

Discussion Questions

» What are the most common types of conflicts you see in school between people?

» What are the most common types of conflicts you see at home between your family members?

» What do you think is the most important group rule we have and why?

Conflict Resolution

Conflict Scenario

Prakash and Genaro are ninth graders. Prakash's other friends, middle schoolers Pete and LeRoy, told him that Genaro wants to fight him this weekend. Prakash doesn't know if this is true or just a rumor, but he sees Genaro in the hallways and Genaro gives him strange looks. Prakash is tired of all the drama and decides to deal with it once and for all. Genaro is walking to the bus when Prakash angrily runs over to him.

Prakash: Jerk, why are you talking about me and mean mugging me?

Genaro: What? What's your problem?

Prakash: I heard you said you wanted to fight me. Well, tell me to my face. Let's fight!

Genaro: What are you talking about? You better check yourself or you will have a fight!

Prakash: (Gets in Genaro's face.) Let's go! Let's do this!

Genaro: You better shut up! (He shoves Prakash.)

Prakash punches Genaro in the arm and they start to fight. The bus driver runs out of the bus, breaks up the fight, and walks the boys over to the assistant principal's office. Both students are sent to the alternative school for 30 days for fighting.

Discussion Questions

1. What was the conflict in this situation?

2. Describe each boy's body language and tone of voice.

3. What were the consequences of the way the boys handled their conflict with each other?

4. How could the boys have handled their conflict without a fight?

5. What would you have done differently in the situation?

The Four Steps of Conflict Resolution

1. Ignore.

2. Walk Away.

3. Say an "I" Message.

For example:

I don't like it when you yell at me, so please stop.

I don't like it when you write mean things about me on Facebook, so don't do it again.

I feel annoyed when you touch my desk, so stop touching it.

4. Tell an adult who can help you solve the conflict.

Conflict Cards

Directions: Cut up these cards and put them in a jar to use in the session seven role-playing scenarios.

You are in math and another student calls you a punk.

Your little cousin keeps coming in your bedroom when you are trying to practice your instrument for band.

A mean kid in class takes something of yours.

Your friend tells you that another student wants to fight you in the bathroom at lunch.

A kid in the hallways bumps into you without apologizing, making you spill all of your things.

Another student has taken your seat on the bus.

Your ex-best friend posts nasty things about you on social media.

The principal accuses you of doing something you didn't do.

The teacher tells you that you can't be in her class without your ID on. You think wearing your ID is stupid.

Your friend returns your phone to you, but it is broken.

A girl in your class keeps spreading rumors about you.

The class bully pushes you off your chair.

Boys' Voice
Session Eight: Reflections and Wrap Up

Topic Overview

The group member will:

» Practice mindfulness with the *Mindful Minute* Activity

» Discuss his success with his goal

» Reflect on his learnings/experiences with the group

» Evaluate the group experience

» Review his goal or coping skills knowledge with a game

Materials

» Reproducibles: *Group Experience Evaluation, Pre/Posttest* (from session one), *Cool It* game or *Coping Skills Bingo* (from previous sessions), *Goal Success Sharing Steps* poster (from session two)

» Chart Paper, Markers, Note Cards, a Bell (or tone on your phone), Pencils, Bingo Chips or Pebbles, a Small Prize

» Your selected items from the Appendix in the digital files

Procedures

1. Take attendance on the Group Notes sheet (included in Appendix). Ask group members whether there is anything they want to discuss relating to boy issues; guide them to limit responses/discussions to 5–10 minutes. If you are ending the group here, remind group members that this is the last group session, and briefly discuss plans for the follow-up session, if you will be having one.

2. Show the rules poster (included in Appendix), and have each group member read a rule aloud.

3. Do the *Mindful Minute* Activity (from session three).

4. *Homework Shareout:* Ask group members to share their experiences with using the four conflict resolution steps over the last week when they had a conflict.

5. *Goal Shareout:* Show group members the *Goal Success Sharing Steps* (from session two). Give group members 1 minute to think of a success they had in the past week with their note card goal. Allow each group member to present the steps to the group. If anyone wants to change or add a second SMART goal (and they have achieved their first goal), allow some time for this. Group members can take their note cards home with them today unless you need to make photocopies for a follow-up session.

6. Review with group members all the main points learned during the Boys' Voice sessions. To best facilitate this review, give group members 1 minute to think of the main things they learned in group and then write their responses on chart paper.

7. Hand out the pretest/posttest (from session one) and read it aloud as group members fill in Yes/No for each posttest statement. Make sure group members write answers in the posttest column and don't change any of their pretest answers. Collect and save the completed posttests for data purposes.

8. Complete the *Group Experience Evaluation*. To do this, the group leader reads each evaluation statement aloud while group members write down their response to that statement. Collect and retain the completed evaluations for data purposes.

9. Play *Coping Skills Bingo* (from session two) or *Goals Bingo* from the Additional Activities (included in Appendix).

10. Praise the group members for all of their hard work. Ask whether there is anything more they would like to discuss or any other help they need. Remind them to let you know if they need to meet with you anytime in the future.

Discussion Questions

» How would you rate your feelings about group ending today on a scale of 1-10 with 10 being the best? Explain your rating.

» What is your goal for yourself now that group is over? Why?

» How would you like to continue to be supported by your counselor/leader and the counseling office in the future?

Supplemental Forms and Handouts for Session Eight
(In Appendix in the digital files)

» Group Notes Sheet
» Group Evaluation
» Pre/Post Test
» Group Rules & Consequences
» Group Pass Examples
» Data Analysis
» Additional Activities

Group Experience Evaluation

Date: _____

Congratulations on completing this Boys' Voice group program! Making changes in your life and setting goals for yourself is hard work, but the success you experience as a result of accomplishing goals feels awesome. Please take a few minutes now to reflect on what you've learned in group and then answer the following questions.

1. What have you learned about yourself through our group experience?

_____

_____

_____

2. How will these learnings affect you in the future?

_____

_____

_____

3. Would you recommend this group to a friend? Why or why not?

_____

_____

_____

4. Which group activity did you find most useful?

_____

_____

_____

5. Which group activity did you find least useful?

_____

_____

_____

6. What did you learn about other people during the group experience?

_____

_____

_____

7. Additional Comments:

_____

_____

_____

References

If you would like to learn more about any of the strategies or activities in this counseling guide, please refer to the sources below.

American Psychological Association. "Boys Don't Cry." Online video clip. *YouTube*. October 6, 2016. Web. Accessed March 1, 2017.

"ASCA Mindsets & Behaviors for Student Success: K-12 College- and Career-Readiness Standards for Every Student." Accessed March 14, 2017. https://schoolcounselor.org/asca/media/asca/home/MindsetsBehaviors.pdf.

"Blood and Leather- Recreating the Masai War Shield. Accessed 4-13-2017. http://www.conserventures.org/news/2012/10/31/blood-and-leatherre-creating-the-maasai-war-shield.html.

American School Counselor Association. (2019). *The ASCA National Model 4th Ed.* Alexandria, VA: author.

Child Mind Institute. "Angry Kids: Dealing with Explosive Behavior." Accessed April 10, 2017. https://childmind.org/article/angry-kids-dealing-with-explosive-behavior/.

"Conflict Resolution." Accessed March 22, 2017. http://www.ncpc.org/topics/conflict-resolution.

Crayola.com, http://www.crayola.com/.

Dckids.com, http://www.dckids.com/.

"How to Make an Authentic Medieval Coat of Arms." Accessed 4-13-2017. http://www.yourchildlearns.com/heraldry_activity.htm.

Kaffenberger, Carol. Making Data Work. 3rd ed. Alexandria, VA: American School Counselor Association, 2013.

Marvelkids.com, http://www.marvelkids.com/.

McCormac, Mary E. "Address Student Anxiety." *ASCA School Counselor*, September 1, 2016. https://www.schoolcounselor.org/magazine/blogs/september-october-2016/address-student-anxiety.

Moninger, Jeannette. "10 Relaxation Techniques That Zap Stress Fast." Accessed April 2, 2014 http://www.webmd.com/balance/guide/blissing-out-10-relaxation-techniques-reduce-stress-spot?print=true.

The Present. Dir. Jacob Frey. Filmakademie Baden-Württemberg, 2014.

Prince Ea. "I am NOT Black, You are NOT White." Online video clip. *Youtube*. November 2, 2015. Web. Accessed June 3, 2016.

Sklare, Gerald. Brief Counseling That Works: A Solution-Focused Approach for School Counselors and Administrators. 2nd ed. Thousand Oaks, CA: Corwin, 2004.

"Taking Charge of Anger." Accessed April 12, 2017. http://kidshealth.org/en/kids/anger.html?WT.ac=k-ra.

Tough Guise: Violence, Media, and the Crisis in Masculinity. Dir. Sut Jhally. Media Education Foundation, 1999.

Boys' Voice Appendix

Forms (in the digital files)

» Parent Permission Letter

» Group Notes Sheet

» Group Evaluation

» Pre/Post Test

» Group Rules & Consequences

» Group Pass Examples

» Data Analysis

» Additional Activities

Parent Permission Letter

Date: _____

Dear Parent/Guardian:

The Comprehensive School Counseling Program at _____ School includes small group counseling sessions. Your child _____, has been referred for participation in one of these counseling groups. With your permission, your child will attend group counseling on a scheduled basis at school by the school counselor. These group sessions will focus on the topic of _____. The sessions will not change the child's academic program. Participation in the group is voluntary, and confidentiality will be discussed in group and respected.

At times, the school counselor and school-based staff (principal, assistant principal, social worker, psychologist, behavior specialist, teacher, nurse, etc.) will need to exchange information about your child (goals, strategies, etc.). All communication will take place only on an educational need-to-know basis.

This permission is for the school year _____.

If you would like for your child to have small group sessions with the school counselor, please sign and return this form to the counseling office.

If you have any questions or concerns, please call _____.

Thank you,

_____
School Counselor

I grant permission for _____ to participate in small group counseling sessions with the school counselor.

_____
Parent Signature

_____
Phone Number

Boys' Voice Pre/Posttest

Name: _____   Date: _____

PRETEST: YES –OR– NO/I DON'T KNOW	Statements	POSTTEST: YES –OR– NO/I DON'T KNOW
	I know what each letter stands for in a SMART goal.	
	I can list five peaceful ways to solve problems with other people.	
	I can name all the steps to conflict resolution.	
	I am successful in school.	
	I can calm myself down when I am upset.	
	I can explain the masculine stereotype.	

Group Rules & Consequences

{ Group Rules }

Only say helpful comments.

Don't tell others what is said in the group.

One person talks at a time; there are no side conversations.

Use the bathroom before or after group only.

Name-calling is not allowed.

Don't touch someone else's stuff.

If you arrive late, bring a pass with the time/an adult signature.

{ Consequences }

Private Warning

Removal from Group

Group Pass Examples

Get your lunch at 11:15 and bring it to the counselor's office to eat TODAY at 4th period.

Come to the counselor's office TODAY at 12:30.

Come to room 504 TODAY during PE. Please bring this pass.

Additional Activities

As mentioned in the recommendations section, these are additional activities for extending or replacing certain sessions.

Some parts of these additional activities may need modification for very young group members. If necessary, the group leader might read aloud while young group members follow along with their finger. In addition, young group members might dictate to the group leader when necessary (for example with four additional leadership qualities) rather than writing on their own.

Coloring Mandala

Superheroes & Villains

This activity can be done as a group with a mural-like activity or done individually with each group member drawing on their own piece of construction paper. Start by having the boys fold the paper in half and draw a line down the fold. Then they can draw and color their favorite superhero on one side of the fold line. Alternately, you can provide illustrations of superheroes that the boys can cut out, color, and glue onto the construction or mural paper. For this option, type in "free superhero coloring pages" into any search engine and choose from all the options there. Some of my favorite sites for coloring pages are dckids.com, marvelkids.com, and crayola.com. Next have students draw and color (or cut out, color, and glue) their favorite villain on the opposite side of the fold line. Finally, hang the paper on the wall and show the boys the following discussion questions to foster a discussion about leadership qualities and what qualities make someone a superhero versus a villain.

Discussion Questions

» What are some of qualities that the superheroes on the paper have in common?

» What qualities do the villains have in common that you all drew (or glued to the paper)?

» Which of the superhero qualities are also qualities that a leader like your teacher or school principal or state governor have?

» What are the most important qualities that a leader should have?

» What leadership qualities do YOU have? What leadership qualities would you like to acquire?

Dear Boys' Voice Experts

Advising others is a great way to apply and practice knowledge learned! Because group members are now "experts" on most boy issues, they will have a chance to help other boys with their problems. Pair up group members and hand out one of the *Dear Boys' Voice Experts* problems below to each pair. Give pairs 5–10 minutes to use their knowledge gained from group sessions, as well as their own life experiences, to find a solution for their fellow male sufferer. Then have each pair read the problem aloud and tell the group what advice they would give to their male writer.

To expand this activity for more practice with using the four steps to resolving conflict, review the *Four Steps of Conflict Resolution* with the group members. Tell your group members to imagine that the writers of the bolded problems below are really struggling with conflict resolution and they need to see their conflict acted out with the four steps of conflict resolution. Then have the group members role-play how to solve each of the highlighted problems below using the four conflict resolution steps.

» **Whenever I get mad, I just want to fight. What do I do?**

» My dad says I have to play a sport in high school because "that's what real men do." I hate sports and want to take dance class. What do I do?

» **Every day another kid cuts me off in the lunch line. I tried to ignore it but it keeps happening. What do I do?**

» I am failing reading and math! I really want to pass my classes! How can I fix this?

» I get so nervous before a test that I almost throw up! What can I do to feel better during a test?

» **The student who sits next to me in science keeps kicking my chair every day. I'm ready to turn around and smack him.**

» **My homeroom teacher falsely accused me of talking when it was my neighbor talking. I'm so mad I don't even want to go to her class anymore.**

» **My little sister comes in my room and messes up my stuff. How do I handle this without getting in trouble from my mom?**

Masculine Shield

In various African countries, such as Tanzania, tribes make special shields for boys entering adulthood. These shields are treasured by the family where they are handed down from generation to generation, with each new owner re-decorating the shield. Have your group members make their own masculine shield; they can decorate their shields with drawings or cutouts of their favorite objects and then color it with their favorite color.

Have the boys select a shield shape, sketch it on butcher paper, and cut it out. Alternately, to save time or if your group members are very young, you can provide a shield template that they can all trace on the paper and then cut out; you might even provide members with their actual shields so all they have to do is decorate it. Once group members have their shields, they should each choose four different symbol printouts, which they can find in magazines and cut out. The symbols should be anything they feel represents them like an animal, sport, hobby, etc. Then have the members color the background of their shield according to what colors symbolize their character traits (see list). Finally, glue the symbols down in each corner. You can either hang the boys' shields up in the group room as is or mount them on construction paper first for more sturdiness. Once the shields are displayed on the group room wall, foster a discussion about how our shields represent us as individuals and challenge the masculine stereotype!

Gold/Yellow – Generosity
Silver/White – Peace or Sincerity
Red – Strength
Blue – Truth or Loyalty
Green – Hope, Joy, or Love
Black – Grief
Purple – Justice
Orange – Ambition
Maroon – Patience

If your group members are older and need a more mature twist on this activity, have them do a few minutes of Internet research on the Medieval Coat of Arms, which was the image or icon of each family that decorated their shields, flags, etc. Alternately you can do the Coat of Arms Internet research yourself and then read the information aloud to the group members. The members can use their newfound knowledge to choose symbols (shapes, stripes, chevrons, objects, etc.) and colors that hold certain meanings for their own history and reputation, and create their masculine shield accordingly.

Row, Row, Flip Your Boat

Divide the group into 2 teams. Give each team a large piece of butcher paper that will serve as the team "boat." All group members should stand on their team's boat. Tell the students to imagine that they are in their boat on a choppy ocean, but that their boat has flipped over with the last big wave and they must get it turned back over or it will sink. Their goal is to flip the boat back upright without anyone falling into the ocean. They can use their hands, but no one can step off the paper or they will be lost in the ocean and the team loses. The team that flips its boat over first without anyone falling into the ocean is the winner!

Goals Bingo

Hand out blank Bingo cards (included in session two) and have group members fill in the bolded part of each goal achievement tip in any mixed-up order on their card. Group members can use beans or pebbles as game pieces. First, call out a Bingo letter and a goal achievement tip. Second, repeat the Bingo letter and goal achievement tip. The first group member to get five beans/pebbles placed in a row or column calls out "BINGO" and wins a prize. After someone wins, have group members clear their cards of game pieces and start again. Collect the Bingo cards after the game to be handed out again for a future game if you are having a follow up session. Alternatively, if you are short on time or your group members are very young, you can give out pre-printed bingo cards.

Goal Achievement Tips

» Always **set goals** for yourself!

» Make sure your goal is **specific**.

» You should have a way to **measure** your goal to know if you achieved it.

» Your goal should be **reasonable** and attainable enough that you can achieve it.

» You goal should be important to you and **relevant** to your life.

» It is important to have a set **time period** for when you will achieve your goal.

» **Post** your goal in your room or phone or binder where you will see it and remember it every day.

» Talk to your **family** about your goal.

» Talk to your **friends** about your goal.

» **Attend** school daily.

» Be **respectful**.

» Follow school **rules**.

» Ask for **help** when you need it.

» Do your **homework**.

» **Participate** in class.

Stretch It Out!

This is a fabulous relaxation exercise that uses stretching and movement to calm the group members and channel their high energy. Start off the exercise by having group members stand with their arms at their sides, feet about shoulder width apart. Tell them you will be leading them in stretching out some of the major muscle groups. Lead them very slowly and carefully through each of the following stretches:

Head/Neck

» Slowly drop your head, chin to chest and then raise it back up again.

» Gently lean your heads back, then raise it back up again.

» Now, turn your head so you are looking over your left shoulder, then back to front, and then looking over your right shoulder, then back to the front.

» Finally, tilt your head until your right ear is near your right shoulder and then raise it back up. Switch sides and repeat so your left ear tilts near the left shoulder and then is raised back up.

» Repeat the above steps 4 more times.

Back

» Gently and slowly walk your fingers down your left side 3 finger-walk strides. Return to upright position.

» Repeat with your right side. Return to upright position.

» Put your hands on either side of the small of your back and gently lean backwards slightly. Return to upright position.

» Repeat the three above steps 4 more times.

Sides

» Raise your right arm towards the sky over your head. Slowly stretch it to the left over your head, bending left slightly at the waist, palm facing the sky. Return to the starting position and repeat gently and slowly 4 more times.

» Repeat these same steps with your left arm, tilting right over your head and bending right slightly at the waist.

Legs

» Stand with your feet shoulder-width apart.

» Lean forward and stretch your arms to the ground, pointing your hands to the space between your ankles, then slowly straighten back to your upright position.

» Again lean forward, this time pointing your hands to your right foot then slowly straighten back to your upright position.

» Finally lean forward, this time pointing your hands to your left foot then slowly straighten back to your upright position.

» Repeat the 3 above stretches 4 more times.

Am I a Leader?

Start this activity by handing out My Leadership Qualities (on the following page) and having each group member complete it. Then, ask the members to make a list of four more qualities that they think are important in a leader. Next have the group combine all their qualities into one leadership quality list, written on chart paper. Use the following discussion questions to foster a discussion about leadership from the qualities listed on the chart paper.

Discussion Questions:

» Pick the leadership quality from the chart list that is most important, in your opinion, and give two reasons why it is the most important leadership quality for you.

» Think about your personal leadership qualities compared to the group list on chart paper. Which chart paper qualities do you have now? Explain.

» Which chart paper qualities would you like to develop? Why do you think you don't have these leadership qualities now?

» Pointing to all the qualities written on chart paper, ask members: Is this the kind of leader you want to be? Why or why not?

» What leadership qualities do you all have in common with each other?

» How can you help each other build the leadership qualities that each boy wants to develop?

My Leadership Qualities

Leadership Quality	I absolutely have this quality.	I have some of this quality.	I do not have this quality.
Positive Attitude- I have a lot of enthusiasm, I stay positive and inspire others to be positive.			
Communication Skills- I can talk to people in a way that gets my point across and I am a good listener.			
Consistency- I show up every day with the same goals and drive to get a project done.			
Collaborative- I work well with other people, no matter who they are. I am good at inspiring others to work together to complete a task.			
Reliable- I do what I say I will do and make sure my tasks get completed.			
Solutionist- I am good at identifying what we need to do to solve a problem or get a job/project finished.			

Four other leadership qualities that I think are important:

1. _____

2. _____

3. _____

4. _____

BE COOL!
Anger Management Group Counseling Guide

{ Table of Contents }

{ Be Cool! Appendix }

Reproducible letters, forms, assessments and other materials contained in the digital files

- » Parent Permission Letter
- » Group Notes
- » Group Evaluation
- » Pre/Posttests
- » Group Rules & Consequences
- » Group Pass Examples
- » Data Analysis
- » Additional Activities

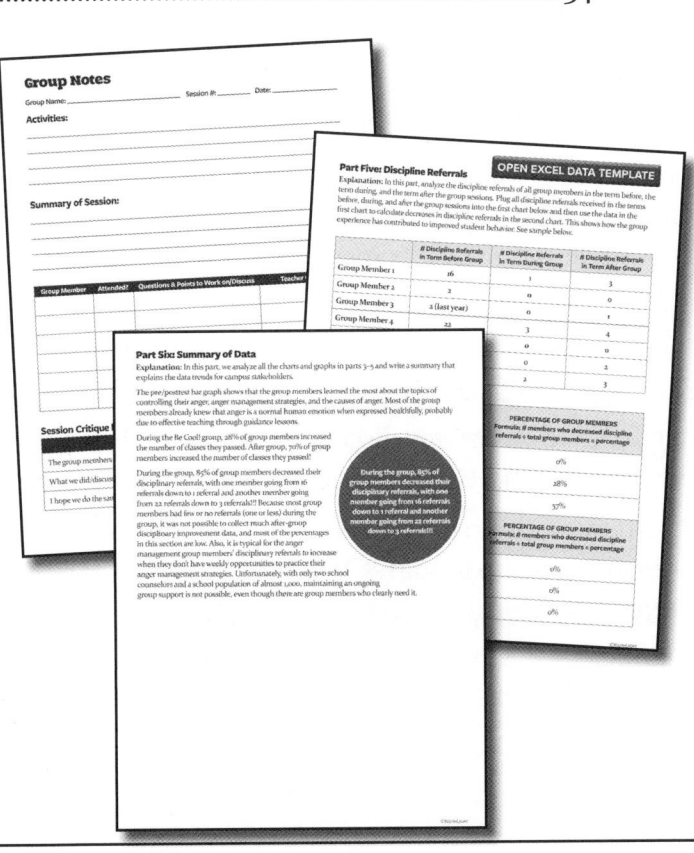

Recommendations Specific to Running an Anger Management Counseling Group

In my years as a counselor, I have found anger management groups to be the most challenging and rewarding to facilitate. This makes sense because the personality of the group often reflects the characteristics of the group theme, so the vibe in anger management groups tends to be high-energy, strong-willed, and well … angry. For this reason, it is best to consider running an anger management group after you already have some experience in running other types of counseling groups. Despite the challenges of anger management groups, I also find them to be the most heartwarming to facilitate! Often, I observe group members' eagerness and enthusiasm to do the right thing mixing with their lack of social skills—often leading to inappropriate, yet comical, comments.

I remember the time years ago when a sixth-grade group member (let's call him Screech) with a huge heart but particularly weak social skills tried to bond and empathize with a fellow group member (we'll call him Zach). Zach was detailing how his anger had landed him in the In School Suspension room for the third time that week. Suddenly, Screech abruptly interrupted Zach with, "Hey man, I do dumba** things all the time, too!" After a startled, brief silence, I questioned, "So, how do we feel about that comment and language?" This turned into a teachable moment as the group agreed that the comment was well-meaning, but we needed to review the group rules. These vulnerable, bull-in-the-emotional-china-shop moments are touching in that they show how desperately group members want to do the right thing and be accepted, despite all their missteps. So, in order to manage this and help group members get the most out of the group experience, I offer the following recommendations.

> Sometimes group members are resistant to participating in role-play exercises. It is important to get everyone involved in role-playing so they can practice their anger management skills in a safe, non-angry environment.

» Though I have included eight sessions (as with all my group guides), I find that anger management group members often max out at six sessions. As a result, I generally wrap up the group experience after six sessions by skipping sessions six and seven and ending with the activities of session eight.

» It is best to keep anger management groups very small due to their challenging nature- four to six members is an ideal number of group participants.

» Have scrap paper available every session for group members to use when they need to express energy and frustrations during discussion/activities. I recommend handing out the paper after the rules review so you have the undivided attention of the group during this part of the session.

» Also have warmup puzzles for group members to do as they are waiting for others to enter and the group session to start. Children in this type of group are usually high energy and can often become irritable if they have to sit around and wait for the group activities to get started. A fun and motivating puzzle is a great wait to start off the group session on a positive note. You can find entertaining anger-themed puzzle worksheets for free all over the Internet, especially at Pinterest. com.

» Sometimes group members are resistant to participating in role-play exercises. It is important to get everyone involved in role-playing so they can practice their anger management skills in a safe, non-angry environment. Here are some ways to get resistant group members involved in role-playing:

- Gently introduce the role-play strategy to the entire group by having the group first read and discuss the role-playing situations/scenarios together and discuss. Alternately they can watch short video clips related to anger and then role-play very brief scenarios that relate to the topics in the video clip. See the Additional Activities (included in Appendix) if you would like more information on video skits or PSAs.

- Tell group members they will vote on the best role-playing at the end of the group session and that all the actors in the role-playing skit that receives the most votes will get a prize.

- Try giving resistant group members pre-written role-playing skits that highlight their particular anger management strategy so they can read aloud and follow their lines. This allows them to focus on practicing their strategy without the distraction of having to think through and act out an improvisation. If you have one group member for whom none of the above strategies works, meet with them privately after group to explore the reason and find a solution, such as individual counseling.

» For group members who have a disciplinary referral/problem that relates to their anger management strategy, it may be best to set up an individual session to facilitate more intensive role-playing so they can practice applying their strategy to the disciplinary referral/problem situation. In these cases, have the group member repeatedly apply their anger management strategy to the referral/problem situation, which you recreate for them. For example, if the group member had a problem with blowing up at someone kicking their chair, I might kick their chair while they practice using their strategy instead of blowing up.

» When time allows, play the game *Cool It!* (included with session three) for about 5–10 minutes at the end of each session. This game leaves the group members with a positive feeling about the group so that they look forward to attending the next session. In addition, the game helps them to become familiar with each of the anger management strategies.

» I often have a follow-up session about a month or two after the group ends to check in on group members' experiences/successes with anger management. To do this, I send group members a photocopy of their last anger management strategy note card one week before the follow-up group so they can have a reminder to practice it. Then, during the follow-up session, I generally repeat the session five steps. At this time, I also compile and analyze the After Group data (included in Appendix).

American School Counselor Association Standards Alignment

The American School Counselor Association (ASCA) sets the national framework for a model school counseling program. As a result, the Be Cool! session activities are aligned with the following ASCA Mindsets & Behaviors that can be applied to the domains of Academic Development and Personal/Social Development.

Mindsets

M 1.	Belief in development of whole self, including a healthy balance of mental, social/emotional and physical well-being
M 5.	Belief in using abilities to their fullest to achieve high-quality results and outcomes
M 6.	Positive attitude toward work and learning

Behaviors

B-SMS 1.	Demonstrate ability to assume responsibility
B-SS 1.	Use effective oral and written communication skills and listening skills
B-LS 2.	Demonstrate creativity
B-SMS 2.	Demonstrate self-discipline and self-control
B-SS 2.	Create positive and supportive relationships with other students
B-SS 4.	Demonstrate empathy
B-SMS 5.	Demonstrate perseverance to achieve long- and short-term goals
B-SS 6.	Use effective collaboration and cooperation skills
B-SMS 7.	Demonstrate effective coping skills when faced with a problem
B-SS 7.	Use leadership and teamwork skills to work effectively in diverse teams
B-SS 8.	Demonstrate advocacy skills and ability to assert self, when necessary
B-SMS 9.	Demonstrate personal safety skills
B-SS 9.	Demonstrate social maturity and behaviors appropriate to the situation and environment
B-SMS 10.	Demonstrate ability to manage transitions and ability to adapt to changing situations and responsibilities

Be Cool!
Session One: All About Anger

Topic Overview

The group member will:

» Make introductions with other members

» Identify the purpose of the group

» Discuss group rules/norms

» Identify some basic tips/strategies related to anger management

Materials

» Reproducibles: *Draw Your Anger, Anger Tips*

» Scrap Paper and Pencils

» Your selected items from the Appendix in the digital files

Procedures

Reminder – These session procedures will take about 1 hour to complete, so feel free to shorten or lengthen the session according to your time constraints. For ideas on how to do this, see the Recommendations for Starting a Counseling Group located at the beginning of this book. Of course, the more experienced you are with facilitating groups and with using this group curriculum, the more efficiently and quickly you will be able to guide group members through the procedures below.

1. Take attendance on the Group Notes sheet (included in Appendix). Provide the warmup activity, *Draw Your Anger,* for prompt group members; other members often trickle in slowly during the beginning of the first group session because it's a new routine for them.

2. Tell group members that the purpose of the group is to learn and practice ways to calm their anger and express it in healthful ways. Show the rules poster (included in Appendix), and have each group member read a rule aloud and share what he/she thinks the rule means. Remember to always remind group members that they can say "pass" if they do not want to read aloud or share. Additionally, as mentioned in the recommendations section, it's always good to have scrap paper available in every session for group members to use when they need to express energy and frustrations. I recommend handing out the paper after the rules review so you have the undivided attention of the group during this part of the session.

3. Have students introduce themselves by giving their name, grade, and favorite calming activity. You should go first to model this for group members.

4. Hand out the group member pretest (included in Appendix), and read aloud as group members fill in Yes/No for each statement. Collect and save these pretests until the last group session.

5. Hand out an *Anger Tips* sheet to each group member (Appendix D) and read it in a round-robin fashion. You can also add a movement aspect to this activity, which is often needed by group members struggling with anger issues. Let group members actively show their response to the *Anger*

Tips by stepping forward if they think an *Important Anger Fact* is true and standing still if they think the fact is false; in the same vein, members can step forward if they've tried a *Managing Anger* strategy or stand still if they haven't tried it. After the group has finished reading, ask group members on which tips they need further explanation. Group members should take these sheets home to share with family and display in a prominent place.

6. Optional Homework Activity: Instruct group members to do the following, "As you're spending time with people over the next week, notice what things you're doing to handle your anger if you get mad. Think about what works best to calm you down when you're angry. We'll talk about this during the next session."

7. Complete the group evaluation (included in Appendix). To do this, read each evaluation statement aloud while group members hold up fingers to indicate whether they agree with/disagree with/feel "sort of" about each statement. Then tally group members' responses in each Agree/Sort of/Disagree column on the Group Notes sheet (included in Appendix) for use in planning the next session.

Supplemental Forms and Handouts for Session One
(In Appendix in the digital files)

» Parent Permission Letter

» Group Notes Sheet

» Group Evaluation

» Pre/Post Test

» Group Rules & Consequences

» Group Pass Examples

» Data Analysis

» Additional Activities

Discussion Questions

» What was the most surprising "Important Anger Fact" in your opinion? Why?

» What is your favorite way to manage anger? Why is it your favorite?

» How do you think people will have problems if they express their anger in a violent way?

Draw Your Anger Warmup

A warmup puzzle or activity is a great way to start off the group session on a positive note. I recommend providing an optional warmup worksheet for group members at the beginning of every session. You can find really good anger-themed puzzle worksheets and mandalas for free all over the Internet, especially at Pinterest.com. Here is one of my own warmups to start you off....

When you're angry, you feel one way. Then when your mood changes and you're feeling calm, you feel a different way. Draw a picture below showing your anger feeling and your calm feeling.

ANGER

CALM

Anger Tips

Important Anger Facts

Anger is a normal human response, and everyone has it.

Problems come from unhealthy ways of expressing anger.

Feeling sick or tired makes it easy to get angry.

YOUR THOUGHTS make you angry, not other people or events.

The best time to control your anger is when it begins.

If you don't control your anger, it can get worse.

People can hurt themselves/others when they get mad.

Managing Anger

Tell someone how you feel.

Relax and take deep breaths.

Get away from the situation that is making you angry.

Exercise to burn off your anger.

Know you have a choice in how you express anger; think of the different choices you have.

Know your choice will lead to a consequence; think of the consequences of what you do.

You Will Have Problems if You

Break something

Hit or kick people or animals

Yell in anger

Break rules at school/work or home

Be Cool!
Session Two: Choosing Your Anger Management Strategy

Topic Overview

The group member will:

» Learn about nine anger management strategies and choose the one that works best for them

» Role-play their chosen anger management strategy

Materials

» Reproducibles: *Anger Management Strategies, Goal Prompt Template*

» Note Cards, Cardstock, Scrap Paper, Pencils

» Your Selected items from the Appendix in the digital files

Procedures

1. Take attendance on the Group Notes sheet (included in Appendix). Ask group members whether there is anything they want to discuss relating to anger management issues; guide them to limit responses/discussions to 5–10 minutes (see the recommendations section for tips on keeping within these time constraints).

2. Show the rules poster (included in Appendix), and have each group member read a rule aloud. Remember to always remind group members that they can say "pass" if they do not want to read aloud.

3. Ask group members to share what things calmed them down when they felt angry over the last week. Hand out an *Anger Management Strategies* sheet to each group member and read it in a round-robin fashion. After the group has finished reading, ask group members on which numbers they need further explanation.

   Note: For best results, copy the *Anger Management Strategies* sheet on red cardstock because group members will use it in each session. After each session, collect the photocopies of this sheet and pass them out again in the following session.

4. Group members should pick their favorite anger management strategy from the *Anger Management Strategies* sheet and write it on a note card, using the *Goal Prompt Template*. You should model this first by using the prompt to copy your favorite anger management strategy on a note card.

5. Each group member reads their anger management strategy note card aloud to the group.

6. Each group member role-plays the anger management strategy on their note card, with you acting as the instigator (who/what) who makes that student angry. For example, ask "Who wants to practice their strategy with me?" Then ask the volunteering group member, "What makes you angry at school?" If the group member says, "Kids who kick my chair make me angry," then gently kick the group member's chair while coaching them to act out the anger management strategy on their note card. Be sure to spend a minute or two after each role-play briefly discussing how their strategy could be applied in a classroom setting.

7. Collect the note cards and *Anger Management Strategies* sheets. (Photocopy the note cards after group and give the originals to group members as a reminder to practice their preferred anger management strategy during the week. Keep the photocopies for the next group session.) Praise group members for their efforts.

8. Optional Homework Activity: Instruct group members to do the following, "As you're spending time with people over the next week, practice your chosen anger management strategy when you feel mad. Pay attention to how/whether your strategy calms you down and keeps you out of trouble. We'll talk about this during the next session."

9. Complete the group evaluation (included in Appendix). To do this, read each evaluation statement aloud while group members hold up fingers to indicate whether they agree with/disagree with/feel "sort of" about each statement. Then tally group members' responses in each Agree/Sort of/Disagree column on the Group Notes sheet (included in Appendix) for use in planning the next session.

Supplemental Forms and Handouts for Session Two

(In Appendix in the digital files)

» Group Notes Sheet

» Group Evaluation

» Group Rules & Consequences

» Group Pass Examples

» Data Analysis

» Additional Activities

Discussion Questions

» Is having a goal in your life important? Why or why not?

» Do you consider your anger management strategy to be a goal? Why or why not?

» What anger management strategy did you chose today? Why did you choose that strategy?

Anger Management Strategies

How do you handle your anger??

Circle the anger management strategy that will work best for YOU!

1. Take time out and relax.
Count to ten. Take five deep breaths. Feel yourself go all rubbery.

2. Walk away from the problem.
Go to a safe place.

3. Write or draw your feelings on paper.
Make pictures or words showing how you feel.

4. Use humor. Make a joke out of it.
Think of something funny about what happened or laugh at yourself.

5. Think: it's no big deal. Convince yourself to LET IT GO!
Decide if the problem is worth getting upset over.

6. Talk it out. Use "I" messages.
Tell the person/group how you feel OR tell them to stop in a serious way.

7. Say you are sorry and make up.
Only do this if you really mean it.

8. Get help from an adult.
Or ask another student to mediate.

9. Make a list of bad consequences of you getting angry.
Read the list to calm yourself and control your anger.

Goal Prompt Template

For best results, copy the Goal Prompt on a large, laminated, colored piece of paper because it will be hung on the wall for group members to use as a model in every session.

Goal Prompt:

When I'm angry, I promise to try to:

_____

_____

_____.

Be Cool!
Session Three: Success with Anger Management

Topic Overview

The group member will:

» Role-play their chosen anger management strategy

» Discuss their success with their anger management strategy

» Learn that anger can cause illnesses

Materials

» Reproducibles: *Anger Causes Illness, Anger Management Cards, Anger Management Strategies* (from last session), *Goal Success Sharing Steps, Goal Prompt Template* (from last session), *Cool It! Game*

» Note Cards, Scrap Paper, Pencils, Dice, Jar or Small Box

» Your selected items from the Appendix in the digital files

Procedures

1. Take attendance on the Group Notes sheet (included in Appendix). Ask group members whether there is anything they want to discuss relating to anger management issues; guide them to limit responses/discussions to 5–10 minutes (see the recommendations section for tips on keeping within these time constraints).

2. Show the rules poster (included in Appendix), and have each group member read a rule aloud. Remember to always remind group members that they can say "pass" if they do not want to read aloud.

3. Read *Anger Causes Illness* and discuss briefly.

4. Hand out the photocopies of the anger management strategy note cards and *Anger Management Strategies* sheets from the last session. Have group members read the anger management strategies aloud in a round-robin fashion to review.

5. Show group members the *Goal Success Sharing Steps* and model how to do steps 1 and 2. For example, you can read off, "When I'm angry, I promise to try to use an 'I' message to talk it out" from your anger management strategy note card from the last session. Then you can tell group, "When my sister told me that I didn't cook a tasty dinner, I told her 'I feel sad and unappreciated when you tell me that the dinner I worked hard to cook isn't tasty.'"

6. Give group members 1 minute to think of a success they had in the past week with the anger management strategy on their note card.

7. Allow each group member to present their *Goal Success Sharing Steps* to the group. Ask group members if they feel their anger management strategy is working to calm their anger or if they need to pick a different strategy.

8. Have group members write their same anger management strategy on a new note card OR pick a different strategy from their *Anger Management Strategies* sheet and write it on a new note card, using the *Goal Prompt Template* from last session. You should model this first by using the prompt to copy your favorite anger management strategy on a note card.

Supplemental Forms and Handouts for Session Three

(In Appendix in the digital files)

» Group Notes Sheet

» Group Evaluation

» Group Rules & Consequences

» Group Pass Examples

» Data Analysis

» Additional Activity

9. Each group member reads their anger management strategy note card aloud to the group.

10. Each group member role-plays the anger management strategy on their note card, with you acting as the instigator (who/what) who makes that group member angry (see session two for an example of this, if necessary). Because this session may run long, it is fine to have half the group do their role-playing today and the other half do their role-playing during the next session.

11. Collect the note cards and *Anger Management Strategies* sheets. (Photocopy the note cards after group and give the originals to group members as a reminder to practice their preferred anger management strategy during the week. Keep the photocopies for the next group session.)

12. Optional Homework Activity: Instruct group members to do the following, "Talk to your family about the anger management strategy you're using. Tell them how it's working for you, and ask them what strategy calms them down. We'll talk about this during the next session."

13. If there is time, play *Cool It!* with group members.

14. Complete the group evaluation (included in Appendix). To do this, read each evaluation statement aloud while group members hold up fingers to indicate whether they agree with/disagree with/feel "sort of" about each statement. Then tally group members' responses in each Agree/Sort of/Disagree column on the Group Notes sheet (included in Appendix) for use in planning the next session.

Discussion Questions

» How do you feel about role-playing your anger management strategy? Explain.

» How did you feel when you learned that anger can cause cancer and heart disease? Why did you feel this way?

Anger Causes Illness

Anger is a normal human feeling that all people have. When people limit their angry responses and express anger calmly, it can actually be a very useful emotion. But did you know that getting angry a lot can hurt the inside of your body?? Now we're not talking about stubbing your toe when you kick something in anger or getting a bloody nose if you are in a fight—we all KNOW of those ways that anger can hurt us. But, did you know that feeling angry repeatedly for long periods of time can damage your heart, your stomach, and your intestines; increase your blood pressure, etc.? There have been many studies throughout the world in the last 100 years showing that people who are more angry have more health problems. Specific studies have shown that angry people are twice as likely to develop heart disease and have higher rates of cancer. One of the reasons for this is that people have increases in blood pressure and heart rate when they are angry, and our bodies can't handle these increases if they happen too often. Another reason for this is that anger and stress can lead to inflammation that, over many years, can cause cancer. So even if you aren't getting in trouble at school/work, or fighting with people, your body, your health, and your HEART are still suffering from anger!

Discussion Questions

1. How could anger hurt your body?

2. What kinds of illnesses are caused by repeated anger?

3. Why do you think anger hurts your body?

4. What part of this reading surprised you? Why?

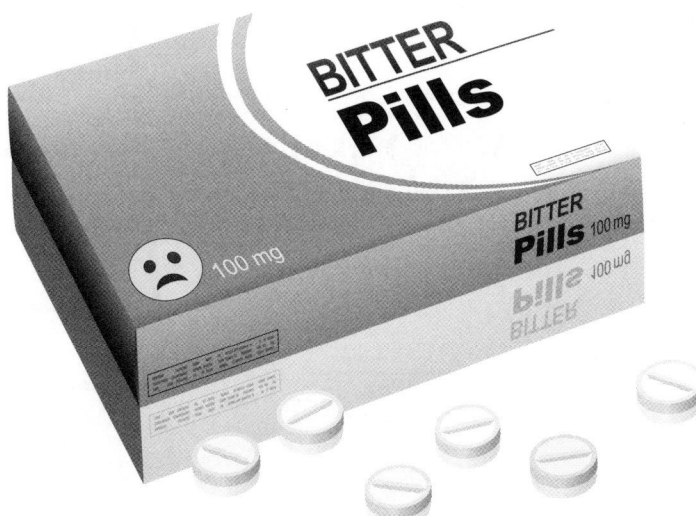

Goal Success Sharing Steps

For best results, copy the *Goal Success Sharing Steps* on a large, laminated, colored piece of paper because it will be hung on the wall for group members to use as a model in every session.

Goal Success Sharing Steps:

1. Read your goal aloud.

2. Give an example of your success with the goal.

Cool It! Game

Materials:

Anger Management Strategies (cut out the strategies on the next page so that each strategy is on an individual slip of paper), decorated box, set of dice, chips (optional)

Directions:

① Fold the slips of paper showing the anger management strategies and put them in the box.

② With group members standing in a circle, have a group member take one strategy from the box and roll the dice.

    a. If they roll an even number, they must give an example of a time that they used the strategy and how they felt as they used it. If the group member has never used the strategy, they can describe a situation where they might use it in the future.

    b. If they roll an odd number, the group member on their right must give an example.

    c. If they roll doubles, the entire group must discuss the strategy and share their experiences with using it.

③ After the first group member has taken their turn, have the next group member take a turn, moving in a clockwise position.

④ Continue playing until everyone has had two or three turns.

⑤ If group members can handle it, give them a chip each time they are able to give an example of a time they used the strategy or would use the strategy in the future. This really motivates them to rack their brains and talk about their successes with anger management strategies. The group member with the most chips at the end of the game can win a small prize.

Anger Management Cards

Take time out and relax.	Make a joke out of it.
Count to ten.	Laugh at yourself.
Take five deep breaths.	Tell them to stop in a serious way.
Feel yourself go all rubbery.	Make up with the person.
Walk away from the problem.	Distract yourself by talking to a friend.
Go to a safe place.	Write your feelings on paper.
Ask another student to mediate.	Use humor.
Get help from an adult.	Say you're sorry.
Think about how it's no big deal.	Tell how you feel.
Convince yourself to LET IT GO!	Use "I" messages.
Make angry pictures showing how you feel.	Think of something funny about what happened.
Make a list of bad consequences of you getting angry.	Read your consequences list to calm yourself and control your anger.

Be Cool!
Session Four: You Can't Make Me Mad

Topic Overview

The group member will:

» Role-play their chosen anger management strategy

» Discuss their success with their anger management strategy

» Learn that their thoughts cause their anger

Materials

» Reproducibles: *What Causes Your Anger?, Anger Management Strategies* (from last session), *Goal Success Sharing Steps* (from last session), *Goal Prompt Template* (from last session), *Cool It! Game* (from last session)

» Note Cards, Scrap Paper, Pencils, Dice, Jar or Small Box

» Your selected items from the Appendix in the digital files

Procedures

1. Take attendance on the Group Notes sheet (included in Appendix). Ask group members whether there's anything they want to discuss relating to anger management issues; guide them to limit responses/discussions to 5–10 minutes (see the recommendations section for tips on keeping within these time constraints).

2. Show the rules poster (included in Appendix) and have each group member read a rule aloud. Ask group members to share the highlights of their discussion with family members about their preferred anger management strategies.

3. Read *What Causes Your Anger?* and discuss briefly.

4. Hand out the photocopies of the anger management strategy note cards and Anger Management Strategies sheets from the last session. Have group members read the anger management strategies aloud in a round-robin fashion to review.

5. Show group members the *Goal Success Sharing Steps* from the last session and model how to do steps 1 and 2. For an example of this modeling, see session three.

6. Give group members 1 minute to think of a success they had in the past week with the anger management strategy on their note card.

7. Allow each group member to present their *Goal Success Sharing Steps* to the group.

8. Have group members write their same anger management strategy on a new note card OR pick a different strategy from their *Anger Management Strategies* sheet and write it on a new note card, using the *Goal Prompt Template* from last session. You should model this first by using the prompt to copy your favorite anger management strategy on a note card.

9. Each group member reads their anger management strategy note card aloud to the group.

10. Each group member role-plays the anger management strategy on their note card, with you acting as the instigator (who/what) who makes that group member angry (see session two for an example of this, if necessary). Alternately, if you feel group members are ready and can handle this, you can teach them how to role-play in pairs. Be very careful, making sure that group members clearly understand how to choose a less-upsetting anger stimulus and to act it out gently as the instigator. To teach them to role-play with a partner, you can select one generic anger stimulus (for example, giving mean looks or pointing without touching) and then have each pair role-play for the group while you carefully monitor their interaction. As always, remember to spend a minute or two after each role-play briefly discussing how their strategy could be applied in a classroom setting.

If this group session runs long, it is fine to just role-play with the group members who didn't get to role-play last week.

11. Collect the note cards and *Anger Management Strategies* sheets. (Photocopy the note cards after group and give the originals to group members as a reminder to practice their preferred anger management strategy during the week. Keep the photocopies for the next group session.)

> ## Supplemental Forms and Handouts for Session Four
> (In Appendix in the digital files)
> » Group Notes Sheet
> » Group Evaluation
> » Group Rules & Consequences
> » Group Pass Examples
> » Data Analysis
> » Additional Activities

12. Optional Homework Activity: Instruct group members to do the following, "Share the information you learned from the reading *What Causes Your Anger?* with a family member. We'll talk about this during the next session."

13. If there is time, play *Cool It!* (from last session) with group members.

14. Complete the group evaluation (included in Appendix). To do this, read each evaluation statement aloud while group members hold up fingers to indicate whether they agree with/disagree with/feel "sort of" about each statement. Then tally group members' responses in each Agree/Sort of/Disagree column on the Group Notes sheet (included in Appendix) for use in planning the next session.

Discussion Questions

» How do thoughts, and not people, cause your anger?

» How did you feel when the kid in the *What Causes Your Anger?* story realized that it was a kindergartener that bumped into him?

» How is your anger management goal working or not working for you so far? Explain.

What Causes Your Anger?

So, what causes YOU to get angry? Is it: Your friends? Your teachers? Hard schoolwork? Your parents? Your brother or sister? Mean looks? When someone yells at you?

The answer is NO! None of the things above can make you angry; only you can make yourself angry. You might think that sounds crazy, but let's look at an example. Imagine that one day you're waiting quietly outside your teacher's door for the bell to ring. You're minding your own business, not bothering anyone. All of a sudden, someone bumps into the back of you, stepping all over the backs of your feet! How would you feel? Angry, right? But then you turn around and see that it's a kindergartener who got away from his mom and is running around, lost and scared, in your school. How would you feel now? You'd probably want to help the little guy, right? So you see, it's not someone bumping into you that made you mad...it was YOUR THOUGHTS about getting bumped that made you mad! You still got bumped, but your thoughts about getting bumped changed when you turned around and saw it was a scared kindergartener. You thought, "let me help him" rather than "that jerk pushed me," and so you felt bad for the kindergartener rather than mad at him. And this is great, great news: if your thoughts cause your anger then you always have total control over your anger. You CAN control your anger. So let's say it all together now...what makes you angry? YOUR THOUGHTS!

Discussion Questions

1. How do thoughts cause anger?

2. Why would someone bumping you make you angry *(hint - what do you THINK when they bump you)*?

3. Why would you feel less or no anger if the person who bumped you was a helpless little kid?

4. What could you do to manage or calm your anger if you know thoughts cause anger?

Demanding Thoughts

Thoughts that make people angry are called Demanding Thoughts, such as "I demand that you show me respect" or "That teacher better give me an A." If you demand something that you have no control over (like someone else's actions), then you are setting yourself up to be angry. What are some less demanding words you can tell yourself if you start to feel angry?

Now, let's take a moment to replace our "demand" words in our thought with "wish " words because wish words don't make us angry. For example:

"You should..." --instead: *"I wish you would..."*

"I demand..." --instead: *"I'd like..."*

"He better stop..." --instead: *"I would feel better if..."*

Now, let's practice using these wish words instead of your demand words. Everyone can think of one demand sentence and then turn it into a wish sentence. Say both out loud to the group so we can see if you are able to do it!

In school and at home, practice using these wish words instead of your demand words and see if that helps you reduce your anger.

Be Cool!
Session Five: Practice Makes Perfect

Topic Overview

The group member will:

» Role-play their chosen anger management strategy

» Discuss their success with their anger management strategy

Materials

» Reproducibles: *Anger Management Strategies* (from last session), *Goal Success Sharing Steps* (from last session), *Goal Prompt Template* (from last session), *Cool It! Game* (from session three)

» Note Cards, Scrap Paper, Pencils, Dice, Jar or Small Box

» Your selected items from the Appendix in the digital files

Procedures

1. Take attendance on the Group Notes sheet (included in Appendix). Ask group members whether there is anything they want to discuss relating to anger management issues; guide them to limit responses/discussions to 5–10 minutes.

2. Show the rules poster (included in Appendix), and have each group member read a rule aloud. Remember to always remind group members that they can say "pass" if they do not want to read aloud.

3. Ask group members to share their family members' reactions to *What Causes Your Anger?* (from last session). Ask them, "What makes you angry?" to which they should all answer, "Your thoughts." Prompt this answer from last session's reading, if necessary. Hand out the photocopies of the anger management strategy note cards and *Anger Management Strategies* sheets from the last session.

4. Show group members the *Goal Success Sharing Steps* (from last session) and model how to do steps 1 and 2. For an example of this modeling, see session three.

5. Give group members 1 minute to think of a success they had in the past week with the anger management strategy on their note card.

6. Allow each group member to present their *Goal Success Sharing Steps* to the group.

7. Have group members write their same anger management strategy on a new note card OR pick a different strategy from their *Anger Management Strategies* sheet and write it on a new note card, using the *Goal Prompt Template* from last session. You should model this first by using the prompt to copy your favorite anger management strategy on a note card.

8. Each group member reads their anger management strategy note card aloud to the group.

9. Each group member role-plays the anger management strategy on their note card, with you acting as the instigator (who/what) who makes that group member angry (see session two for an example

of this, if necessary). Alternately, if you feel group members are ready and can handle this, you can teach them how to role-play in pairs. See session four if you need tips on this.

10. Collect the note cards and *Anger Management Strategies* sheets. (Photocopy the note cards after group and give the originals to group members as a reminder to practice their preferred anger management strategy during the week. Keep the photocopies for the next group session).

11. Optional Homework Activity: Instruct group members to do the following, "Ask a friend to tell you about any changes they have seen in you since you started the Be Cool! group. We'll talk about this during the next session."

12. If there is time, *Play Cool It!* (from session three) with group members.

13. Complete the group evaluation (included in Appendix). To do this, read each evaluation statement aloud while and group members hold up fingers to indicate whether they agree with/disagree with/feel "sort of" about each statement. Then tally group members' responses in each Agree/Sort of/Disagree column on the Group Notes sheet (included in Appendix) for use in planning the next session.

Supplemental Forms and Handouts for Session Five
(In Appendix in the digital files)

» Group Notes Sheet
» Group Evaluation
» Group Rules & Consequences
» Group Pass Examples
» Data Analysis
» Additional Activities

Discussion Questions

» In your opinion, what is the most important thing that you have learned in group so far? Why is this important to you?

» How will you be able to use this important knowledge that you've learned in group in your future?

» What have you learned about others in our group?

Be Cool!
Session Six: Riding the Anger Wave

Topic Overview

The group member will:

» Complete an art project that shows their chosen anger management strategy applied to their anger triggers

» Gain the insight that using their anger management strategy can influence others' behavior

» Discuss their success with their anger management strategy

Materials

» Reproducibles: *Ocean Wave Art Project, Anger Management Strategies* (from last session), *Goal Success Sharing Steps* (from last session), *Goal Prompt Template* (from last session)

» Note Cards, Scrap Paper, Pencils, Drawing Paper, Colored Pencils or Markers

» Your selected items from the Appendix in the digital files

Procedures

1. Take attendance on the Group Notes sheet (included in Appendix). Ask group members whether there is anything they want to discuss relating to anger management issues; guide them to limit responses/discussions to 5–10 minutes.

2. Show the rules poster (included in Appendix), and have each group member read a rule aloud. Remember to always remind group members that they can say "pass" if they do not want to read aloud.

3. Ask each group member to share their friend's observations of how they have changed since starting the Be Cool! group. Briefly discuss the cyclical nature of behavior change—that when we change our own behavior, others around us react to this and change their behavior. You might give group members the following example: if a student with discipline problems starts to follow the rules in class and starts being nicer to the teacher, the teacher will start to change their behavior toward the student (for example, no longer getting mad at the student because the student is no longer breaking any rules or being rude).

4. Hand out the photocopies of the anger management strategy note cards and *Anger Management Strategies* sheets from the last session. Have a group member model steps 1 and 2 of the *Goal Success Sharing Steps* (from last session). Allow each group member to share their goal success by presenting the steps to the group. If anyone wants to change their anger management strategy, have them write their new strategy on a new note card, using the *Goal Prompt Template* from the last session. For all group members keeping the same anger management strategy, just collect their old note cards after finishing the art project below.

5. Have group members complete the following *Ocean Wave Art Project*. After everyone finishes, let group members present their drawings and share what anger management strategy they use to ride their anger wave.

6. If there is time, have group members role-play the anger management strategy on their note card, working in pairs. See session four if you need tips on this.

7. Collect the note cards and *Anger Management Strategies* sheets. (Photocopy the note cards after group and give the originals to group members as a reminder to practice their preferred anger management strategy during the week. Keep the photocopies for the next group session).

8. Optional Homework Activity: Instruct group members to do the following, "We discussed how our changes in behavior cause others to change their behavior. Over the next week, watch your teachers, parents, or peers to see if using your anger strategy has caused others to change. We'll talk about this during the next session."

9. Complete the group evaluation (included in Appendix). To do this, read each evaluation statement aloud while group members hold up fingers to indicate whether they agree with/disagree with/feel "sort of" about each statement. Then tally group members' responses in each Agree/Sort of/Disagree column on the Group Notes sheet (included in Appendix) for use in planning the next session.

Supplemental Forms and Handouts for Session Six
(In Appendix in the digital files)
» Group Notes Sheet
» Group Evaluation
» Group Rules & Consequences
» Group Pass Examples
» Data Analysis
» Additional Activities

Discussion Questions

» Which adult do you think will be most likely to notice how you have changed your behavior to manage your anger better? Why do you think this adult will notice your behavior changes more than other adults in your life?

» Which student do you think will be most likely to notice now that you are changing your behavior to manage your anger better? What changes will this student notice the most, in your opinion?

» In addition to an ocean wave, can you think of another object that represents your anger? Describe how this object represents your anger.

Ocean Wave Art Project

Directions: Hand out blank paper to group members and tell them to draw themselves in an ocean on top of a wave of anger. They should write whatever it is that makes them mad inside the wave. Then they should write their anger management strategy next to themselves on the wave. Discuss with group members the importance of staying on top of and managing their anger like they would ride on top of a wave. Discuss the alternative, which is letting their anger control and crash over them just like the wave would if they don't stay on top of it. Make sure to first model a drawing showing your anger triggers and anger management strategy (see example drawing below) so group members understand how to complete the drawing. After everyone finishes, let group members present their drawings and share what anger management strategy they use to ride their anger wave.

I Walk Away from the Problem

Yelling
Being Tired
Accusations
Interruptions

Be Cool!
Session Seven: Advising Others

Topic Overview

The group member will:

» Apply their knowledge of anger management strategies by advising other group members on how to manage their anger

» Discuss their success with their anger management strategy

Materials

» Reproducibles: *Dear Be Cool! Experts, Anger Management Strategies* (from last session), *Goal Success Sharing Steps* (from last session), *Goal Prompt Template* (from last session), *Cool It! Game* (from session three)

» Note Cards, Scrap Paper, Pencils, Dice, Jar or Small Box

» Your selected items from the Appendix in the digital files

Procedures

1. Take attendance on the Group Notes sheet (included in Appendix). Ask group members whether there is anything they want to discuss relating to anger management issues; guide them to limit responses/discussions to 5–10 minutes. Discuss with the group that the next session will be the last scheduled session. Tell group members that they can meet with you individually on an as-needed basis and give them the procedures for requesting this. In addition, ask them whether they would like a follow-up group session in one month and if so, schedule it. See the recommendations section at the beginning of this guide for tips and suggested content for the follow-up session.

2. Show the rules poster (included in Appendix), and have each group member read a rule aloud. Remember to always remind group members that they can say "pass" if they do not want to read aloud.

3. Ask group members to share their own observations of how others' behaviors toward them have changed since they started the Be Cool! group. Again, briefly review the cyclical nature of behavior change—that when we change our own behavior, others around us react to this and change their behavior.

4. Hand out the photocopies of the anger management strategy note cards and *Anger Management Strategies* sheets from the last session. Have a group member model steps 1 and 2 of the *Goal Success Sharing Steps* (from the last session). Allow each group member to share their goal success by presenting the steps to the group. If anyone wants to change their anger management strategy, have them write their new strategy on a new note card, using the *Goal Prompt Template* from the last session. For all group members keeping the same anger management strategy, just collect their old note cards after finishing the following *Dear Be Cool! Experts* activity.

5. Tell the group that because they are now experts on anger management strategies, they will have a chance today to advise other students on anger issues. Pair up group members and hand out an

anger scenario from *Dear Be Cool! Experts* to each pair. Give pairs 5–10 minutes to use their *Anger Management Strategies* sheets, as well as their own ideas, to find a solution for their fellow anger sufferer. Then have each pair read their anger scenario aloud and tell the group what advice they would give to the writer to solve the anger problem.

6. Collect the note cards and *Anger Management Strategies* sheets. (Photocopy the note cards after group and give the originals to group members as a reminder to practice their preferred anger management strategy during the week. Keep the photocopies for the next group session).

7. Optional Homework Activity: Instruct group members to do the following, "We've used our *Anger Management Strategies* sheets a lot in this group to find the best anger management strategies for ourselves. Now that our group is ending soon, we need to find a way to keep reviewing this sheet so that we keep practicing our anger strategies. Think about how you'll remember to use your *Anger Management Strategies* sheet during difficult times. For example, you might keep it on the bedside table to read each night before bed, post it on the bathroom mirror to read each morning while brushing your teeth, or put it in your smartphone as a daily reminder. We'll talk about this during the next session."

> ## Supplemental Forms and Handouts for Session Seven
> (In Appendix in the digital files)
> » Group Notes Sheet
> » Group Evaluation
> » Group Rules & Consequences
> » Group Pass Examples
> » Data Analysis
> » Additional Activities

8. Let group members vote on whether they'd like to play the *Cool It!* game (from session three) or role-play their anger management strategy. Proceed with the activity that the group chooses. Alternately, if group members would like to try something new, you can substitute one of the additional activities (included in Appendix) for the *Cool It!* game or the role-playing activity.

9. Complete the group evaluation (included in Appendix). To do this, read each evaluation statement aloud while group members hold up fingers to indicate whether they agree with/disagree with/feel "sort of" about each statement. Then tally group members' responses in each Agree/Sort of/Disagree column on the Group Notes sheet (included in Appendix) for use in planning the next session.

Discussion Questions
» How are you feeling about group ending next session? Explain.
» Did you like being an anger management expert in the *Be Cool! Experts* activity? Why or why not?
» What would you advise your family member to do if they were struggling with anger problems?

Dear Be Cool! Experts

Advising others is a great way to apply and practice knowledge learned! Because group members are now "experts" on anger management strategies, they will have a chance to help others deal with their anger. Pair up group members and hand out one of the *Dear Be Cool! Experts* scenarios below to each pair. Give pairs 5–10 minutes to use their Anger Management Strategies sheet, as well as their own ideas, to find a solution for their fellow anger sufferer. Then have each pair read the scenario aloud and tell the group what advice they would give to the angry writer.

Dear Be Cool! Experts,

I have a terrible temper. Whenever someone looks at me with a mean face or laughs at me, I think they're making fun of me, and this makes me furious! I either yell at them or want to fight. Please help me find a way to control my anger and ignore these looks!

Help,

Mean Mugged in Miami

Dear Be Cool! Experts,

Every day there's this kid in my math class who makes fun of me in front of her friends. I've tried to ignore her, but I'm getting really enraged about this issue and I'm afraid I might snap one day! What should I do?

Yours truly,

Snappy

Dear Be Cool! Experts,

I got in a fight last week with my enemy, and now we both have to go to the alternative school for a 30-day placement! I know we'll be in the same classroom because there are only a few kids there (I've been there before). My anger keeps getting me in trouble, and I'm afraid this will continue when I have to be in the same classroom as my enemy. What can I do to solve this problem and stay out of trouble?

Sincerely,

Fightin' Mad

Dear Be Cool! Experts,

I REALLY hate going to spend weekends with my dad in New York City. I can't stand his girlfriend who lives with him and bosses me around. Also, it's really hard to switch to a different routine and home every weekend, especially in a city so loud and busy. This situation is making me madder and madder. I used to be able to just keep my feelings to myself, but I can't anymore. What should I do?

From,

The Mad Hatter in Manhattan

Dear Be Cool! Experts,

I have a really bad habit in class: I talk back and get defensive any time a teacher accuses me of something. This happens even when it's my fault! I think I'm so used to getting in trouble at home that I always have an angry answer ready when the teacher calls me out at school. Help!

Sincerely,

Not the Teacher's Pet

Dear Be Cool! Experts,

I'm having a problem with my brother. He goes in my room and gets into my stuff and then when I get mad and yell at him, he goes crying to our mom. My mom likes him better because he's the baby and she always takes his side. How do I handle this annoying kid?

From,

Oh Brother

Be Cool!
Session Eight: Reflections and Wrap Up

Topic Overview

The group member will:

» Reflect on their learnings/experiences with group

» Evaluate the group experience

» Discuss their success with their anger management strategy

Materials

» Reproducibles: *Group Experience Evaluation, Anger Management Strategies* (from last session), *Goal Success Sharing Steps* (from last session), *Goal Prompt Template* (from last session), *Cool It! Game* (from session three)

» Note Cards, Scrap Paper, Pencils, Chart Paper, Markers, Dice, Jar or Small Box

» Your selected items from the Appendix in the digital files

Procedures

1. Take attendance on the Group Notes sheet (included in Appendix). Ask group members whether there is anything they want to discuss relating to anger management issues; guide them to limit responses/discussions to 5–10 minutes.

2. Show the rules poster (included in Appendix), and have each group member read a rule aloud. Remind the group that this is the last group session, and briefly discuss plans for the follow-up session, if you will be having one.

3. Ask group members to share their ideas about what they will do with their *Anger Management Strategies* sheet (from last session) so that they remember to use their chosen anger management strategy during difficult times. Ask group members a final time, "What makes you angry?" to which they should all answer, "Our thoughts." Hand out the photocopies of the anger management strategy note cards and *Anger Management Strategies* sheets from the last session; group members can take the sheets home with them at the end of the session. Have a group member model steps 1 and 2 of the *Goal Success Sharing Steps* (from last session). Allow each group member to share their goal success by presenting the steps to the group. If anyone wants to change their anger management strategy, have them write their new strategy on a new note card, using the *Goal Prompt Template* from the last session. Group members can take their note cards home with them at the end of the session unless you need to make photocopies for a follow-up session.

4. Review with group members all the main points learned during the Be Cool! sessions. To best facilitate this review, give group members 1 minute to think of the main things they learned in group, then have them write or share their ideas while you write their responses on chart paper.

5. Hand out the group member pretest/posttest (from session one) and read it aloud as group members fill in Yes/No for each posttest statement. Make sure group members write answers in the posttest column and don't change any of their pretest answers. Collect and save the completed posttests for data purposes.

6. Complete the *Group Experience Evaluation*. To do this, read each evaluation statement aloud while group members write down their response to that statement. Collect and retain the completed evaluations for data purposes.

7. *Play Cool It!* (from session three) one last time with group members.

8. Praise the group members for all of their hard work. Ask whether there is anything more they would like to discuss or any other help they need. Remind them to let you know if they need to meet with you anytime in the future.

Discussion Questions

» Rate your feelings about group ending today on a scale of 1-10 with 10 being the best. Explain your rating.

» What is your goal for yourself now that group is over? Why?

» How would you like to continue to be supported by your counselor/leader and the counseling office now?

Supplemental Forms and Handouts for Session Eight

(In Appendix in the digital files)

» Group Notes Sheet

» Group Evaluation

» Pre/Post Test

» Group Rules & Consequences

» Group Pass Examples

» Data Analysis

» Additional Activities

Group Experience Evaluation

Date: _____

Congratulations on completing this Be Cool! group program! Making changes in your life and setting goals for yourself is hard work, but the success you experience as a result of accomplishing goals feels awesome. Please take a few minutes now to reflect on what you've learned in group and then answer the following questions.

1. What have you learned about yourself through our group experience?

_____

_____

_____

2. How will these learnings affect you in the future?

_____

_____

_____

3. Would you recommend this group to a friend? Why or why not?

_____

_____

_____

4. Which group activity did you find most useful?

_____

_____

_____

5. Which group activity did you find least useful?

_____

_____

_____

6. What did you learn about other people during the group experience?

_____

_____

_____

7. Additional Comments:

_____

_____

_____

References

If you would like to learn more about any of the strategies or activities in this counseling guide, please refer to the sources below.

American Psychological Association. "What Makes Children Angry." Accessed May 2, 2017 http://www.apa.org/act/resources/fact-sheets/children-angry.aspx.

American Psychological Association. "How to Recognize and Deal with Anger." Accessed May 2, 2017. http://www.apa.org/helpcenter/recognize-anger.aspx.

"ASCA Mindsets & Behaviors for Student Success: K-12 College- and Career-Readiness Standards for Every Student." Accessed May 8, 2017. https://schoolcounselor.org/asca/media/asca/home/MindsetsBehaviors.pdf.

American School Counselor Association. (2019). *The ASCA National Model 4th Ed.* Alexandria, VA: author.

Corey, M.S., & Corey, G. (2006). *Groups Process and Practice.* Thomson Books/Cole.

Kaffenberger, Carol. *Making Data Work.* 3rd ed. Alexandria, VA: American School Counselor Association, 2013.

KidsHealth, http://kidshealth.org/.

Lukens, E.P., & McFarlane, W. R. (2004). *Psychoeducation as evidence-based practice: Considerations for practice, research, and policy. Brief Treatment & Crisis Intervention,* 4(3), 205-225.

Missouri Professional School Counselors and Counselor Educators. *A Professional School Counselor's Guide to Planning, Implementing & Evaluating School-Based Counseling Groups,* January 2014.

A Model Comprehensive, Developmental Guidance and Counseling Program for Texas Public Schools: A Guide for Program Development, Pre-K-12th Grade. Austin, TX: Texas Education Agency, 2004.

Pinterest, https://www.pinterest.com/.

Schooltube, http://www.schooltube.com/.

Sklare, Gerald B. *Brief Counseling That Works: A Solution-Focused Approach for School Counselors and Administrators.* 2nd ed. Thousand Oaks, CA: Corwin Publishing, 2004.

Wellcast, http://www.watchwellcast.com/.

Be Cool! Appendix Forms (in the digital files)

» Parent Permission Letter
» Group Notes Sheet
» Group Evaluation
» Pre/Post Test
» Group Rules & Consequences
» Group Pass Examples
» Data Analysis
» Additional Activities

Parent Permission Letter

Date: _____

Dear Parent/Guardian:

The Comprehensive School Counseling Program at _____ School includes small group counseling sessions. Your child _____, has been referred for participation in one of these counseling groups. With your permission, your child will attend group counseling on a scheduled basis at school by the school counselor. These group sessions will focus on the topic of _____. The sessions will not change the child's academic program. Participation in the group is voluntary, and confidentiality will be discussed in group and respected.

At times, the school counselor and school-based staff (principal, assistant principal, social worker, psychologist, behavior specialist, teacher, nurse, etc.) will need to exchange information about your child (goals, strategies, etc.). All communication will take place only on an educational need-to-know basis.

This permission is for the school year _____.

If you would like for your child to have small group sessions with the school counselor, please sign and return this form to the counseling office.

If you have any questions or concerns, please call _____.

Thank you,

_____

School Counselor

I grant permission for _____ **to participate in small group counseling sessions with the school counselor.**

_____

Parent Signature

_____

Phone Number

Be Cool! Group Member Pre/Posttest

Name: _____ Date: _____

PRETEST: YES –OR– NO/I DON'T KNOW	Statements	POSTTEST: YES –OR– NO/I DON'T KNOW
	I can control my anger.	
	I know five calming anger strategies.	
	Anger is a normal human feeling.	
	Other people or events can make me angry.	
	Anger can cause heart problems/disease.	

Staff Pre/Posttest

Administer this pre/posttest orally to the group members' teacher/group of teachers; the pretest can be administered one week before the group begins, and the posttest can be administered one week after the group ends. Use the scale below to write a numbered answer to each question. Make additional copies of this page if you have more than five group members.

1 = You see the student/client exhibit the behavior rarely or never   2 = You see the student/client exhibit the behavior monthly
3 = You see the student/client exhibit the behavior weekly   4 = You see the student/client exhibit the behavior daily
NA = not applicable

Name of Student	How often does he/she express anger by assaulting people or objects?	How often does he/she express anger through criticism, sarcasm, insults, or profanity?	How often is he/she unable to reduce or control his/her level of anger?	How often do his/her angry outbursts interfere with relationships with peers/staff?	How often is he/she unable to follow directions?	How often is he/she unable to complete schoolwork?
1. _____						
Pretest						
Posttest						
2. _____						
Pretest						
Posttest						
3. _____						
Pretest						
Posttest						
4. _____						
Pretest						
Posttest						
5. _____						
Pretest						
Posttest						

Group Rules & Consequences

{ Group Rules }

Only say helpful comments.

Don't tell others what is said in the group.

One person talks at a time; there are no side conversations.

Use the bathroom before or after group only.

Name-calling is not allowed.

Don't touch someone else's stuff.

If you arrive late, bring a pass with the time/an adult signature.

{ Consequences }

Private Warning

Removal from Group

Group Pass Examples

Get your lunch at 11:15 and bring it to the counselor's office to eat TODAY at 4th period.

Come to the counselor's office TODAY at 12:30.

Come to room 504 TODAY during PE. Please bring this pass.

Additional Activities

As mentioned in the recommendations section, these additional activities can be used to extend sessions or as replacement activities during sessions.

Some parts of these additional activities may need modification for very young group members. If necessary, you might read aloud while young group members follow along with their finger. In addition, young group members might dictate to you when necessary (for example with the comics) rather than writing on their own.

Read All About It!

If you have time in your sessions, it is wonderful to add 5–10 minutes of read-aloud time to the beginning of the session. Read-aloud time is especially calming for those who are battling anger issues, and it is also an excellent filler activity as group members are entering your group session during the first five minutes of the session. Below is a list of excellent books that include themes of anger management. Also included are some examples of thought-provoking discussion questions in case you would like to explore the book's themes together through discussion.

Titles

Josh's Smiley Faces: A Story about Anger, by Gina Ditta-Donahue

Hot Stuff to Help Kids Chill Out: The Anger Management Book, by Jerry Wilde

How to Take the Grrrr Out of Anger, by Elizabeth Verdick and Marjorie Lisovskis

Cool Down and Work Through Anger, by Cheri J. Meiners

Angry Octopus, by Lori Lite and Max Stasuyk

I Was So Mad (Little Critter), by Mercer Mayer

The Magic Finger, by Roald Dahl and Quentin Blake

The Outsiders, by S. E. Hinton

Lord of the Flies, by William Golding

A Long Way Gone: Memoirs of a Boy Soldier, by Ishmael Beah (This is an excellent and spellbinding memoir but it is too long and too violent to read aloud in its entirety; however, certain parts can be read to show the damaging power of anger.)

Discussion Questions

» What did you learn from the story?

» Does the main character deal with his/her anger healthfully or unhealthfully? How?

» What anger management strategies does the main character use?

» Do you know anyone in your family who expresses their anger unhealthfully? How do you feel about it?

» What is the problem in the story? Tell me about a problem in your life.

» What is the solution? What kinds of solutions do you like?

» Does anyone in the story change? Tell me about someone you know who changed.

This Is How We Do It

Video skits and public service announcements (PSAs) on anger management can be very helpful in showing group members how other people manage their anger in a healthful way. You can follow the video activity steps below to extend your sessions or in place of the role-playing activity in session two or session three until group members get more comfortable with each other and the group experience*. To utilize videos with group members, start by giving a brief synopsis of the video and then ask members for ideas on why they are watching this video in group. Next, show group members the discussion questions below (written on chart paper) so they know what to watch for as they view the video.

Discussion Questions

» What anger management strategy did you see or did the person in the video talk about?

» How was the person able to use their anger management strategy?

» What happened as a result of using their anger management strategy?

» What might have happened if the person hadn't used their anger management strategy?

» What other strategies could they have used instead?

Finally, show the video and talk about the discussion questions. Below are some good resources for anger management video skits or PSAs. All of these videos can be found by typing the full titles into a Web search engine or by going directly to the website listed below and typing the title into the website's own search engine at the top of the webpage.

» Kidshealth.org: "Kids Talk About Bullying" (This video is more about bullying than anger; however, it does address a couple of anger issues related to bullying and how to handle both in healthful ways.)

» Kidshealth.org: "Train Your Temper"

» Schooltube.com: "Anger Management PSA"

» Schooltube.com: "Anger Management, Williston Middle School"

» Schooltube.com: "Anger Management"

» Watchwellcast.com: "Anger Management" (This is a video for older group members; it really isn't appropriate for elementary school group members. You can locate it by selecting All Episodes at the top of the website.)

*If your entire group is uncomfortable with role-playing, it is crucial to spend 5–10 minutes during that session or during the following session discussing what is causing their discomfort. Then spend an additional 10–15 minutes guiding them to the idea that practicing their anger management strategies in a safe, non-angry situation is necessary in order to achieve what they want for themselves: calming their anger in real-life, stressful situations. During this discussion, it is helpful to address how practice situations may feel silly but give us the skills we need to calm ourselves when the stress or conflict is overwhelming. Liken their anger role-playing group practice to how it might feel lining up outside a perfectly safe building on a rainy day for a fire drill. You might also give group members the analogy of a professional athlete's practice leading up to game day; discuss how every professional athlete must spend hours practicing against his/her own teammates each day to prepare for that one- or two-hour game against the competing athlete(s) on game day.

Tear It Up

This art activity is a simple, cathartic project that group members can complete fairly quickly. To start, provide group members with various colors of tissue paper. Let them do some healthy venting by tearing the tissue paper into different shapes- strips, little pieces, etc. Then hand out an 8 × 11 piece of cardstock or construction paper to each group member. Members can glue down their torn tissue paper pieces to make pictures showing how they're feeling. Anyone who would like to can present their artwork to the group.

Calming Strategies

Often people can manage their anger very well by using various calming strategies, such as muscle relaxation or breathing exercises. Below is part of a resource from one of my other guides, *The Unstressables,* that describes various calming strategies and how to use them. Hand out the following list of calming strategies to each group member and read it in a round-robin fashion. Then teach and lead the group in practicing each strategy. The complete version of *The Unstressables* guide can be found in the book, *Get Your Goal On Volume Two.*

Breathing Backward

This breathing strategy is simple and introduces an opposite way of breathing than we are used to— exhale first, inhale second. Follow these steps to learn the Breathing Backward technique:

1. Purse your lips and hold up one finger.

2. Exhale through your mouth with pursed lips while you hold up one finger.

3. Inhale through your nose while you hold up two fingers.

4. Repeat (exhale breath first, inhale breath second) four more times.

Muscle Makeover

This muscle relaxation exercise can be done anywhere, even sitting at your desk during a test! Follow these steps to learn the Muscle Makeover technique:

1. Sit upright in your chair.

2. Scrunch up your entire face like you just smelled something really bad: eyes squeezed shut, mouth puckered, nose crinkled, etc. Hold for 5 seconds and then let your entire face relax into a calm expression. Repeat four times.

3. Clench your fists as tight as you can and hold for 5 seconds, then release. Repeat four times.

4. Push your arms out at about a 35-degree angle from your body, stretching them and reaching down as far as you can. Hold for 5 seconds and then release to let your arms fall gently at your sides. Repeat four times.

5. Push the soles of your feet into the floor as hard as you can, holding onto your chair or desk for leverage. Hold for 5 seconds and release, relaxing your legs. Repeat four times.

6. Curl your toes inside your shoes as tight as you can, holding for 5 seconds. Then release your toes to lie flat in your shoes. Repeat four times.

Vent It!

This calming strategy lets you share your feelings about and experiences with stress and anxiety with another person by using an "I" message. An "I" message is a calmly spoken sentence where the stressed person tells another person how they feel or what they want beginning with the word "I." Find someone you trust who you know cares about you and start up a conversation about your stress to give yourself a chance to vent! Here are the steps to the Vent It! strategy:

1. Think about why you're feeling stressed.

2. Now think of someone you trust and what that person could do to help you feel less stressed.

3. Use an "I" message to tell that person or a group member how you feel.

4. Now tell that person how they can help you or what you'd like them to do. Sometimes the only thing you need is for them to listen. If that's the case, you can tell them that.

Anger Management Squeeze Bag

If your group members want a stress ball to use as an anger management tool and they like to do craft activities, you can add this fun project to your sessions. With the group, define stress and discuss how it relates to anger. Then brainstorm some ways to handle stress with your group members. Ask them how they might use a stress ball or anger management squeeze ball to manage their anger or combat stress in a way that no one around them would even know they have a stress ball or bag. Give each group member a resealable plastic bag and cotton balls. They should stuff their plastic bag with as many cotton balls as possible and then zip it up. Voila, Anger Management Squeeze Bag! If you work with younger group members, this might be a good time to brainstorm appropriate and inappropriate ways to use their squeeze bag. If you work with older group members, you can hand out colored permanent markers so they can draw anger management designs on their squeeze bag.

It's Comical

Comics are a great way to combine art and anger management. Group members can begin this activity by thinking about their favorite funny experience, movie, joke, or story. Then have them draw a comic depicting this humorous topic. Once they've finished, they can display the comic in a prominent place in their home and think of it anytime they start to feel angry. Sources for blank comics can be found all over the Web; just Google "free blank comic" and then take your pick! Alternately, if your group members don't have Internet access during the group session, they can cut out the comics in the local newspaper and replace the text with their own text. Group members can also make their own comics by drawing two to four squares, drawing their own comic characters (or using magazine cutouts) within the squares, and finally filling in the dialogue bubbles with their funny experience! If you have time, have the group members do a "comic walk" where they can view and enjoy each others' comics.

About the Author

Stephanie Lerner is a Johns Hopkins University-trained school counselor. She holds a BS in elementary education and an MS in counseling. With more than 20 years in both public and private education, she has Texas certifications in school counseling and bilingual/Spanish education. After traveling the world and teaching in such far-off places as Mozambique and Bolivia, Stephanie came home to the United States to be a bilingual counselor and teacher in a high-need public school system. She also teaches school counseling university classes in Texas and presents on counseling topics throughout the USA. When she's not writing or counseling, she enjoys ranch life with her husband and their menagerie of pets—all of whom practice healthy coping skills, of course!

For any questions you have related to this book, direct them to Stephanie Lerner at www.schoolcounselorstephanie.com or www.bilinguallearner.com. You can follow Stephanie on her Facebook page, on Instagram, on Twitter, or on Pinterest to receive information about her other upcoming books.

https://www.instagram.com/schoolcounselorstephanie

www.facebook.com/schoolcounselorstephanie

https://www.pinterest.com/schoolcounselorstephanie

www.twitter.com/bilinguallearn